1 & 2 SAMUEL

FOR NORMAL PEOPLE

A Guide to Prophets, Kings,
and Some Pretty Terrible Men

Aaron Higashi

The Bible for Normal People Book Series

1 & 2 SAMUEL FOR NORMAL PEOPLE
Copyright © 2024 by The Bible for Normal People
Published by The Bible for Normal People
Harleysville, PA 19438
thebiblefornormalpeople.com

Library of Congress Cataloging in Publication Data is available upon request.

ISBN: 978-1-964423-02-9 (Print)
ISBN: 978-1-964423-03-6 (eBook)

Cover design: Danny Wong

To my four ladies,
who have taught me how to love
and
To all the fathers
who try to be better than David

TABLE OF CONTENTS

Infomercial

Hi, I'm Aaron, a biblical scholar and university instructor living in the desert wilderness of Arizona (i.e., Phoenix), and I'm incredibly excited to be sharing this book with you. As a Christian with a Jewish family, I've seen the power of the stories in 1 and 2 Samuel and how they've resonated with different communities across time, space, and faith tradition, and I hope to share my passion for these stories with you.

Of all the books in the Hebrew Bible,[1] 1 and 2 Samuel have some of the most well-known characters and some of the least well-known stories. Everyone knows David. Everyone knows Goliath. But hardly anyone can tell you what happens in the other fifty-something chapters of these books.

Do you remember when the ark of the covenant cut off the head of a Philistine god? Do you remember when Samuel led a traveling troupe of prophetic musicians? Do you remember the necromancer? Or the angel of death? Do you remember when David ran a protection racket or when he was a Philistine mercenary?

---

[1] The term "Hebrew Bible" refers to the same texts as the Protestant Old Testament, although as I'll discuss soon, the texts are organized differently. "Hebrew Bible" is the preferred term in academia for the texts because it's more religiously neutral. "Old Testament" presumes a "New Testament" and so is an explicitly Christian term, whereas "Hebrew Bible" refers to the language it was written in.

How about this: do you remember that one time when David stole another man's wife? No, not *that* time, the other time? No, not *that* time either.

Maybe you do.[2] Congrats. But you probably don't, and that's okay. The characters of 1 and 2 Samuel have grown so large in our imaginations that they overshadow the actual stories in which we find them. This can make reading the Bible a disorientating experience, in which we're forced to reconcile the characters as they exist in our minds with the characters as they exist in the text.

While a certain amount of disorientation can be fun—who doesn't love those spinny rides at a theme park?[3]—too much can turn us off reading a story. And that's unfortunate, because 1 and 2 Samuel have some of the Hebrew Bible's best-written characters and most thrilling stories. This is peak biblical storytelling. We're talking *Game of Thrones*.[4] We're talking *The Godfather*.[5] It would be a shame to miss out on all that drama.

That's why this book exists: to help you, a (relatively) normal person, get the most out of your reading of 1 and 2 Samuel. This book will guide you through 1 and 2 Samuel with an eye toward three things: (1) helping you make sense of these stories so you don't miss any shocking or sordid details; (2) putting you in touch with what the best biblical scholarship has to say about these books without overwhelming you with boring stuff; and (3) addressing matters of faith that inevitably arise.

And they'll arise. They'll arise fast because 1 and 2 Samuel are home to some of the most toxic people the Bible has to offer. There are enough walking red flags here to make a parade. As you read about these characters and their ambitions, their violences, and their betrayals, you'll wonder over and over again why characters like these are

---

[2] Don't lie to me.
[3] Me. I don't like them.
[4] Not season eight.
[5] Not number three.

in a text so many people call sacred. Why is God interested in them? Why is God interested in anyone? And while I can't promise definitive answers to every question you might have, we'll work together to find some healthy ways to process all this.

But let's not get ahead of ourselves. We have some time before we meet these characters. Let's start with the basics.

1 & 2 Samuel from 30,000 Feet

Basic Facts

Name and Contents

The books of 1 and 2 Samuel are named after the prophet Samuel, a figure from the 11th century BCE, who was born in a little town called Ramah just a few miles north of Jerusalem. Samuel plays a significant role in some early stories of 1 Samuel but then disappears from the narrative half way through and dies before the end of the book. The books, then, aren't named 1 and 2 Samuel because they're about Samuel, but because they're about the lasting legacy of Samuel's life.

Samuel, you see, appoints the first king and thereby transforms Israel from a loose collection of tribes to a more centralized monarchy. This isn't just a political and economic change, it's also a change in self-identity in terms of how Israel understands itself. This change is accompanied by new theology—or new ways of thinking about God. Both 1 and 2 Samuel chart the glorious rise and tragic fall of the first two kings of Israel. These dramatic arcs are Samuel's legacy and the reason for the books' titles.

There was a time when 1 and 2 Samuel used to be just one book called Samuel. But when the original Hebrew text was translated into

Greek, the story became too large to fit on a single scroll,[1] and it was broken into rough halves. Similar things happened to 1 and 2 Kings, 1 and 2 Chronicles, Ezra and Nehemiah, and the twelve Minor Prophets (Amos, Hosea, Micah, etc.). It would be nice if it was still called Samuel—that's shorter and doesn't jack up my word count—but we don't always get what we want.

Together, 1 and 2 Samuel cover roughly a century's worth of history, from the mid-11th century BCE to the mid-10th century BCE. This is early in the Iron Age for the region of Israel and only shortly after the late Bronze Age collapse that led to the fall of many of the most powerful empires of the day. It's a volatile time period, where new peoples, new technologies, and new ways of life are vying for their time in the sun. The tension between these new ways of life is what drives a lot of the action in 1 and 2 Samuel's stories.

Authorship

Let's talk about authorship. We have absolutely no idea who wrote 1 and 2 Samuel. Tradition held that Samuel himself and other prophets like Gad and Nathan wrote the books, but this tradition doesn't explain why the text is the way it is, and it's disregarded by biblical scholars. We do have a good idea that there wasn't just one author. The material that makes up these books seems to have been written at different times by different people for different reasons and then edited together into the books we have today. There are multiple versions of several stories, as if two separate people started writing on their own and then someone came along later and put the versions together.

Because we can't say for certain who wrote 1 and 2 Samuel, we also don't know when they were written. Biblical scholars who focus on stories about David and the way these stories look like political propaganda might date some parts of these books to near the events they

---

[1] Greek takes up a lot more space than Hebrew because it has weird things like *vowels*.

describe, so around 950 BCE, not long after David's reign is believed to have ended. But biblical scholars who focus on stories that seem to be looking back on events in light of Babylonian captivity might date parts of these books to the middle of the exile, so around 550 BCE. Our authors are scattered throughout that 400-year spread.

That's not a very precise dating range, but it does tell us something significant about the authors. It tells us that, for four hundred years, people born in different times and facing different hardships kept coming back to these stories to expand on them and find new meaning in them for their communities. It's only because of their enduring willingness to find new meaning in old stories that the stories still exist for us to read today.

If you're coming to these old stories to find new meaning in them, then you have at least one small thing in common with the authors. Since we otherwise can't know anything about the authors, it's nice that we can share this.[2]

Canonical Location

In a Protestant Old Testament,[3] 1 and 2 Samuel are the ninth and tenth books, following the book of Ruth and preceding the books of 1 and 2 Kings. But in a Jewish Tanakh,[4] 1 and 2 Samuel are the eighth and ninth books. That's because the book of Ruth is very near the end of a Jewish Tanakh rather than coming after Judges as it does in a Protestant Old Testament. This small difference is worth spending a moment to explain, since it affects the way we think about the books of 1 and 2 Samuel.

---

[2] Basically BFFs.

[3] Catholic, Orthodox, and other denominations of Christians have different numbers of books in their Bibles, though this general schema of organization holds true.

[4] "Tanakh" is the preferred Jewish term for the Hebrew Bible. It's an acronym for the three major sections of the text: Torah, Nevi'im, and Khetuvim.

A Protestant Old Testament and a Jewish Tanakh are similar in content, but the books in their respective canons are each organized differently. A Protestant Old Testament is organized in three sections: Pentateuch, history, and poetry. The Pentateuch is the first five books of the Bible (Genesis, Exodus, Leviticus, Numbers, and Deuteronomy).

The books that follow the Pentateuch are classified as "historical texts," and they tell the story of Israel's conquest of Canaan, the rise of the monarchy, and Israel's eventual defeat at the hands of the Babylonian Empire. Both 1 and 2 Samuel are part of these historical books. The books that come after these historical books are poetry, broadly speaking, and include everything from actual poetry (like the Psalms and Song of Songs) to wisdom literature (like Proverbs) and the prophetic writings (like Isaiah and Amos).

In a Protestant Old Testament, we read Ruth before we read 1 and 2 Samuel. Ruth ends with a brief genealogy revealing that Ruth is an ancestor of David, and so we turn to 1 and 2 Samuel to see a character called David who looks like he's historically destined to rule.

A Jewish Tanakh, on the other hand, is also organized in three sections: Torah (Instruction), Nevi'im (Prophets), and Ketuvim (Writings). The Torah has the same books as the Pentateuch. The books that follow are classified as "prophetic texts"; so Joshua, Judges, 1 and 2 Samuel, and 1 and 2 Kings are treated as prophetic texts, specifically, the "Former Prophets."

This might seem like a strange label if we think of prophetic texts as texts named after a prophet, like Isaiah, Jeremiah, Ezekiel, etc. But it's not a strange label when we remember that there are prophets in many of these books. Jewish tradition holds that Joshua himself was a prophet. Deborah is a prophet[5] in Judges. Samuel, Nathan, and Gad are prophets in the books of 1 and 2 Samuel. And 1 and 2 Kings have the famous prophets Elijah and Elisha.

In the Jewish Tanakh, we go right from Judges to 1 and 2 Samuel, and so we're not primed to look for David like we are when we read

---

[5] Slay queen.

Ruth first. Instead, we are primed to look for the prophets of 1 and 2 Samuel and see what they are going to show us about God. Keeping a close eye on the prophetic characters in the text is not a bad idea, but ignoring the human dimension of the text because we're obsessed with seeing what's going on with God will also cause us to miss the majority of what's happening in the story. That's because 1 and 2 Samuel are not like the stories in the Pentateuch, where God is doing things like speaking from fiery mountain tops, parting seas, writing laws, appearing in person, and having meals with people. God's presence in these stories is, as a rule, subtle, and the relationship between the prophetic characters and God is often as complex as any other characters. Prophets aren't a clear, unobstructed window into the internal life of God, and as a result, we'll have as many questions for them as we have for anyone else.

To summarize: the Protestant Old Testament and the Jewish Tanakh invite us to think of 1 and 2 Samuel in two different ways. Are these historical books to be appreciated for the events they relate? Or are these prophetic texts where we come to learn about the will of God through prophetic figures and their ministries?

In a sense, the answer is "neither," since the people who wrote 1 and 2 Samuel likely had no idea that these books would end up in collections called the Old Testament or Jewish Tanakh. But in another very real sense, the answer is "both," depending on your preferences and the religious communities you may or may not be a part of. You have the freedom as a reader of these texts to get whatever you'd like out of them, and the books themselves can't tell you otherwise. It's entirely possible to come to these books on one occasion in your life and read them as history, only to come back to the books on some other occasion in your life and read them as prophetic. It's entirely possible to never read them as either or to read them as more. Give yourself permission to have a full range of interpretive options in front of you.

Whatever you choose to do, it's also helpful to know that 1 and 2 Samuel is half like a story from Judges and half like a story from 1 and

2 Kings. In the book of Judges, life is characterized by an endless cycle of sin and obedience. The people of Israel sin by worshiping other gods, then God punishes them by having another nation oppress them. The people repent, so God then raises up a judge to lead the people of Israel to victory over their oppressors and give them back their freedom for a time. The cycle repeats: more disobedience, more oppression, more repentance, more judges, more freedom, etc., etc.

Like Judges, 1 and 2 Samuel is a story with a national scope that's often focusing on wars and that's told from the perspective of a handful of influential and divinely inspired leaders. Remember that the judges of Judges are not actual *judges*[6]; rather, they are charismatic freedom fighters who are empowered by God to fight off Israel's oppressors. Samuel himself is a judge, in addition to being a prophet, priest, and seer. He's the last character to have the title of judge, though Saul fits the description, too. Like Judges, cycles of sin and obedience are major drivers of the action and a major subject for the narrator to reflect on in 1 and 2 Samuel.

Like 1 and 2 Kings, 1 and 2 Samuel are primarily stories about kings. These are not ancestral sagas like in Genesis, or national epics like in Exodus. These are stories about what kings do, how they become kings, how they stay kings, and how other people remove them from kingship by violence or duplicity. Fortunately, 1 and 2 Samuel never becomes as dry as 1 and 2 Kings can be, falling into formulaic recitations like "such and such was king for twenty years, did X and Y, then died," but the main characters of the books are similar.

Because 1 and 2 Samuel are stories about kings, they're also political stories. When people are little, they're sometimes told not to talk about politics and religion at the dinner table. To read and make sense of 1 and 2 Samuel, we have to do both. Rude, but necessary. Indeed, the line between politics and religion is virtually non-existent in these stories. The characters who are significant in one way are always significant in the other way as well. We'll have to table our modern tendency

---

[6] Except Deborah, she do be judging.

to think about politics and religion separately if we really want to delve into these texts.

Character and Narrative

Considered as literature, 1 and 2 Samuel is some of the best stuff the Bible has to offer. I want you to try a little thought experiment to illustrate this fact. I want you to picture in your mind, using the vastness of your imaginative powers, what Moses looks like. Go ahead. Do it. What does he look like? Your answer will probably date you based on whichever Exodus movie happened to be popular when you were growing up. For me, Moses looks like Moses does in the Dreamworks *Prince of Egypt* movie because I'm an older millennial. My Moses is an animated Moses and sounds a lot like Val Kilmer. Your Moses may vary.

But whatever your Moses looks like in your head, he doesn't look that way because the Bible describes him that way. The Bible doesn't describe Moses *that way* because the Bible doesn't describe Moses *any way*. Moses is the main protagonist of four books in the Bible, Exodus through Deuteronomy, and never once are we given a physical description of him.

We're also almost never told what Moses is thinking. We see Moses's actions. We're told he does stuff. But the narrator rarely, if ever, tells us what's going on inside Moses's head. We have to infer what he's thinking by using the limited clues we have available to us, and the scenes where such clues are available are few and far between. That's because we rarely get scenes where Moses is doing what *Moses* wants to do. Instead, we get a lot of scenes where Moses does what God tells him to do.

Now perhaps Moses is such a faithful and obedient dude that what God tells Moses to do and what Moses wants to do are identical. Great. But that still doesn't give us any insight into his unique motivations as a character. Who is Moses, really? The books of Exodus through

Deuteronomy aren't written in such a way that we'll ever have a good answer to that question.

This lack of narrative detail is quite common for the Bible. In contrast with contemporary novels, where enriching descriptions are the norm, biblical narratives are sparse and colorless. This sparsity can be interesting, as it invites a reader to fill in the gaps with their own creative imagination, but it also limits how confronting the text can be since the characters in the text are as much a product of our own thoughts as they are of the text itself. When a character is half me to begin with, they can only surprise me so much.

Contrast those stories with the stories in 1 and 2 Samuel. Saul and David have canonical, biblical descriptions. It's not a lot, but it's something. How many characters in the Bible have any physical descriptions at all? Hardly any is the answer you're looking for. More importantly, we spend a lot of time with Saul and David, watching them do what *they* want to do. We see their reasoning, their unguarded ambitions, and their sincere grief concerning a host of issues; and as a result, we have a much clearer understanding of who they are as human beings than we do virtually any other character in the Bible.

I can therefore say with my whole chest that, while Moses is the person in the Bible with the most amount of raw text dedicated to him, David is the most prominent *character* in the Hebrew Bible. David will surprise you, if you pay attention, because David will always be more a product of the text itself than of our thoughts about the text.

Aside from characterization, the literature of 1 and 2 Samuel is sophisticated in other ways. We get descriptions of weapons and equipment; we get complicated plots and political strategy; there are elements of suspense, horror, and tragedy; there are scenes with thrilling action; there are tons of lies and half-truths that you might miss if you don't pay attention, as well as flattery and duplicity, robust dialogue, and a whole lot more. Dramatic features that are infrequent in other stories of the Bible are sprinkled all over 1 and 2 Samuel with reckless abandon, and that makes these stories a particular joy to read.

History and Evidence

Considered as history, 1 and 2 Samuel don't fare quite as well, and you might wonder whether any of the events described in these narratives actually happened. That's hard to say. Both books consistently have a third-person omniscient narrator who has access to the thoughts of multiple characters and the private events they're involved in. That's not the kind of writing that tends to be historical, because historians only have access to publicly available and recorded events. No one person, or even group of people, could have witnessed all of the events described in 1 and 2 Samuel, meaning at least some literary license has been taken with the story.

Having said that, in 1993, archaeologists discovered a piece of writing on a broken Canaanite tablet from the 9th century BCE called the Tel Dan Stele, and the stele mentions the "House of David." This stele seems to attest to the existence of a dynasty named after David, which, at that point, had existed for two hundred years. That's *probably* enough to say a person named David actually existed and actually was king, but it *probably doesn't* tell us anything else.

Was David anointed in a private ceremony by the prophet Samuel (1 Sam 16:13)? Did David and Jonathan undress in front of each other in a private meeting (1 Sam 18:4)? Did David sneak up on Saul when he was alone in a cave, relieving himself? These stories might preserve important and interesting traditions, but it's simply impossible to confirm if they happened historically. As a result, if our appreciation of these books depends on us reading them as history, then it's likely we won't appreciate them much at all.

Summary and Approach

How are we going to tackle these old stories? I'm so glad you[7] asked. First, let me give you a quick summary of what 1 and 2 Samuel are

---

[7] By *you*, I, of course, mean *me*.

about and then they'll make more sense when I explain how these books are divided up.

The book of 1 Samuel opens with a story of Samuel's miraculous birth to his mother, Hannah, who was barren until God's intervention. Samuel is raised as a priest and is shown to have God's favor from an early age, despite Israel's religious leadership being otherwise ineffective and corrupt.

Then, 1 Samuel cuts away from Samuel himself to narrate a story about the Philistines, foreign warriors who have recently settled in the region and have immediately become a threat to the Israelites. The Israelites and the Philistines go to war, and the Israelites bring the ark of the covenant with them, which acts as a symbol of God's presence in battle. Despite the presence of the ark, the Israelites lose the battle, and the ark is captured. Through a series of miracles, however, the ark manages to return itself to the Israelites, and Samuel defeats the Philistines with a miraculous display of power.

The people of Israel, apparently dissatisfied by their dependence on Samuel, ask Samuel to appoint a king to lead them in battle. While Samuel is hesitant, God tells him to go through with it, and Saul is chosen by Samuel as the first king over Israel. Saul is initially successful in his military campaign against the Philistines, but he disobeys Samuel on several occasions, and Samuel moves to replace him by anointing David in a secret ceremony.

The rest of 1 Samuel then describes David's rise to power. David has a swath of military successes of his own, marries into Saul's household, attracts the loyalty of Saul's son, manages to evade Saul's increasingly paranoid attempts to kill him, and eventually winds up as a mercenary for the very Philistines with whom Israel had otherwise been locked in conflict. It's while David is a mercenary that Saul and his eldest son are killed in battle against the Philistines, and David inserts himself into the power vacuum to become king over southern Judah.

The initial chapters of 2 Samuel describe, in terse, blow-by-blow fashion, how all of the people who could contest David's claim to the throne die in rather serendipitous ways. The prophet Nathan then visits David and delivers an unprecedented message from God that David's dynasty will endure forever. David thus becomes king over a united Israel and Judah.

If the story so far has been about David's rise, the remainder of the story recounts David's fall, as the rest of his life is marked by personal evils and family tragedies. David rapes Bathsheba, the wife of one of his elite soldiers, and when she falls pregnant as a result, he has her husband murdered to cover everything up. David's son Amnon, not falling far from the proverbial tree, rapes his half-sister Tamar, leading to a civil war that tears David's household apart and sees him driven from his capital city in disgrace. It's only through the swift action of Joab, David's general and consigliere, that the civil war is put down, and David is able to return to Jerusalem to live out the remainder of his life.

The book of 2 Samuel then ends abruptly and ambiguously. David takes a census in a final bid to secure a legacy for himself, but this has disastrous results. In the last chapter of 2 Samuel, David is still alive, but he is old and impotent. His eldest sons are dead, there's no clear successor to the throne, and the future of his house is painfully uncertain.

The first two chapters of the next biblical book, 1 Kings, step in to give an odd sense of closure. Two rival groups of David's most trusted advisors compete to put two different sons of David on the throne. Nathan and Bathsheba manage to outmaneuver their political opponents and secure Solomon, Bathsheba's son, as king. Their rivals are quickly disposed of, and David's death is finally narrated.

Already in this summary you can probably tell a few things. First, this isn't a happy story. Despite it being a story of nearly endless ambition, virtually no one gets what they want, and by the end it's not clear whether any good has been achieved at all. And second, it's not a very edifying story. You don't walk away from the story feeling as though you have a better understanding of how to be happy, faithful, or moral. You might even begin to ask some difficult questions: what is a story like this doing in the Bible? And what kind of god is God, such that *this* of all things is part of Scripture?

It's my belief that there is a lot of value in this story—literary, moral, and spiritual—but wresting it from the text is going to require us to do some things we might not normally do when we read the Bible: we're going to treat these characters as hostile witnesses. That is to say, we're going to treat these characters like they're trying to hide what they're doing wrong. By closely interrogating their stories with a healthy suspicion, I believe we can learn a lot about God and a good life by simply doing the opposite of what they do.

Since this is a character-focused approach to the material of 1 and 2 Samuel, it's appropriate that our general outline will be character-focused as well. In this book, we'll divide our discussion of 1 and 2 Samuel into three chapters based around the life of David. The first chapter will be called "Before David," and it'll cover 1 Samuel 1–15. The second chapter will be called "David's Rise," and it'll cover 1 Samuel 16–2 Samuel 9. The third and final chapter will be called "David's Fall," and it'll cover 2 Samuel 10–1 Kings 2.

A final note about my approach is appropriate to give here. There are two issues that I'll raise over and over again as we make our way through these texts. Those issues are fatherhood and ambivalence. It might be helpful to know something about me and who I am as the author of this book as I explain those two issues to you and why I'm so obsessed with them.

Fatherhood

The first thing you might want to know is that I'm a father. Because I'm a father, I can't help but notice fathers and portrayals of fatherhood in any text that I read or piece of media that I consume, and the Bible is no exception. When my second child was born, my wife and I experienced a period of postpartum depression, and one of the (largely ineffective) ways that I attempted to cope with that depression was to try to call to mind all the brilliant people I knew from Western intellectual history and the advice that they had given about being a parent.

I thought to myself, "Hey, I'm a university instructor of philosophy, theology, and biblical studies. I know about some of the smartest people who've ever lived and some of the most sage advice ever given. Surely, somewhere in this mass of wisdom, there's some practical advice I can latch onto to make parenting easier."

Turns out there wasn't. Turns out very few important figures from Western intellectual history were fathers, and turns out, of those who were, even fewer were any good at it. History is littered with the corpses of genius-level thinkers who couldn't parent worth a damn. Again, the Bible is no exception. There are plenty of fathers in the Bible. There are plenty of fathers in the stories of 1 and 2 Samuel, Samuel himself included. And yet almost every single father in the Bible is terrible, again Samuel included.

So I'm going to talk about fatherhood a fair amount. When characters are fathers I'll talk about what they're doing and not doing. Even when characters aren't fathers, I'll talk about what they'd be like as fathers, given the evidence we have in the texts. My comments about fatherhood won't be limited to human characters either.

God is portrayed as a father, implicitly in 1 Samuel and explicitly in 2 Samuel. Many people of faith today think of God as a father figure, and Christians worship God the Father as the first person of the Trinity; yet God's fatherhood is as marred as any human character's is in 1 and 2 Samuel. Indeed, many of God's weaknesses as a father resound in the lives of the human characters in the text who attempt to carry out God's will.

As I said before, I'm a father. But to be more specific, I'm a father of three daughters and a feminist besides. So in addition to noticing how people fail to be fathers in these texts, I'm also concerned with how women characters are treated in the text, particularly by men who have power over them. In the Bible, misogyny is not uncommon, but in 1 and 2 Samuel, there are some especially egregious examples of women being mistreated at the hands of men who have absolutely no idea what to do with power beyond replicating the evils of their fathers. I think it would be a failure on my part, as a biblical scholar and as a commentator on these texts, to not point this out when it happens in 1 and 2 Samuel and to not decry it as the moral travesty that it is.

In summary, I hope to persuade you that these stories are enriched when we consider what one generation of characters is handing down to the next, and I also hope to persuade you that we can learn some concrete things about how to be a good parent by doing the opposite of what many characters in the Bible do.

Ambivalence

The second thing you might want to know about me is that I'm writing this book in Phoenix, Arizona, in the early months of 2024. As a result, I'm constantly worried about politics, both foreign and domestic. Because of the magic of books, you can be reading this at literally any point in the future. Amazing, isn't it? You might be sitting in a time and place where there's no need to worry about the 2024 election, where most households in the United States aren't living paycheck to paycheck, where education and healthcare are free, or at least not cripplingly expensive, where systemic racism and rampant misogyny are defeated, where the environment has been saved, and where the market has been forced to serve the common good of everyday people. Maybe you're sitting in a time when there's peace in the Middle East. I can only hope.

But that's not where I'm sitting. I'm sitting in a place where these things are problems. And because I'm a Christian, I think about these problems in both secular policy terms and in Christian theological terms. I wonder, for example, about God's providential role in history. I wonder how best to faithfully serve God and have God's will done on Earth in the midst of nearly endless social and political difficulties.

As I wonder about these things, I find myself ambivalent. I find it difficult to find God in the current moment and to think clearly about God's will. To say it even more simply, I'm not sure what to do, politically or theologically, about a lot of problems we face. I'm deeply conflicted, and then I feel guilty about that conflict, because not everyone in the world has the privilege to sit around feeling conflicted.

To be clear, I have deeply held political beliefs, and I'm ready and willing to act on them. I'm not saying that politics is hard and so we should just throw our hands up and act like it doesn't matter. It does matter. A lot. Especially for vulnerable people. What I'm saying is that I don't have a lot of hope that my deeply held political beliefs can be turned into real policy given the current political landscape. My ambivalence isn't caused by a lack of clarity or conviction in myself but rather by the lack of practical ways to see that conviction realized.

Both 1 and 2 Samuel are ambivalent texts. The stories told in these books are stories where God is difficult to find, where God's will is not clearly revealed, and where people don't know what to do, politically or theologically.

Part of this is because of the multiple authors underneath the surface of the text that I mentioned before. As we read 1 and 2 Samuel, you'll begin to see that one of these authors is very enthusiastic about having a king over Israel, but another author thinks that having a king is a stupid, idolatrous thing for Israel to do. Biblical scholars call these voices the pro- and anti-monarchical sources. Whether they were actual sources that existed independently of one another at some point is not our concern here. We'll simply observe these voices as we come upon them, and we'll really let ourselves feel the ambivalence that arises from having both of these voices back-to-back in the story.

Is having a king a good thing? Both 1 and 2 Samuel spend an awful lot of time developing a theology around having a king, but because they also spend time deriding the possibility of having a king, a reader of these stories can't possibly walk away with a clear answer to that question. The text as it exists today is ambivalent. Having a king might work. Having a king might not. Having a king might be what God wants. It might not. Again, these contrary voices lead to a feeling of ambivalence.

I understand that feeling, because sitting in early 2024, I have that feeling too. Perhaps you have felt that same feeling at some point. Perhaps you're feeling it now. Whatever the case might be, 1 and 2 Samuel are a literary safe haven for people with this feeling. These texts will tell you what God wants, clearly and with conviction, then they will backtrack, hesitate, contradict themselves, and become uncertain as events unfold. The books of 1 and 2 Samuel will oscillate between options and refuse to give a clear answer, not because they don't want to but because, in the face of history's actual complexity, they can't.

Reading the Story

So, how're you feeling?[8] To recap, 1 and 2 Samuel are named for the character whose legacy looms large over these books. We don't know who wrote them or when, but we know different authors in different times kept coming back to these stories over the centuries to find meaning in them. These stories are tragic, but they're also powerfully written, and they have some of the most interesting and toxic characters in the entire Bible.

As we read these stories, we're going to interrogate these interesting characters as though they're hostile witnesses. We're going to bring our skepticism and our condemnations to the table because, frankly, these characters deserve it. And we're going to pry from them insights about how to live good and faithful lives. While we're doing this, we're also going to talk about fatherhood—human and divine—and about the political and theological ambivalence that permeates these stories.

Got all that? I know you do. You're smart and I'm cheering for you. Let's begin.

---

[8] I'm feeling great, thanks for asking.

CHAPTER TWO

Before David

Samuel vs. Eli (1 Samuel 1–3)

The first three chapters of 1 Samuel describe the miraculous birth and blessed childhood of the prophet Samuel. Samuel is born to pious and affluent parents, Hannah and Elkanah, after Hannah struggled to conceive for many years. When Hannah promises to dedicate her future child to God's service, God allows Hannah to conceive, and Samuel is born shortly thereafter.

Samuel is raised in the house of the Lord at Shiloh with the priest Eli and his family, but Eli's sons are greedy, rapacious, and corrupt. An anonymous "man of God" appears and condemns Eli's household, prophesying that his sons and future descendants will die violently.

As Samuel grows to adulthood, he becomes famous all throughout Israel for the visions God gives him, and already by the end of the second chapter we have a subtle suggestion that Samuel will be the one to anoint a future king.

Hannah

The first character we are introduced to in 1 Samuel is Elkanah, but aside from being prestigious enough to warrant a genealogy (1:1), wealthy enough to afford two wives (1:2), and pious enough to make regular pilgrimages (1:3), he is largely irrelevant for the story. The person who is relevant is his beloved wife Hannah, whose name means "grace." Hannah finds herself in the somewhat humiliating situation of being barren, while Elkanah's other wife, Peninnah, has children (1:2). The trope of one wife having children while another doesn't is perhaps most famously narrated in the conflict between Jacob's wives in Genesis 30, but it's no less bitter here, as the only description we get of Peninnah is that she harasses Hannah about her childlessness (1:6).

Hannah's pain from her childlessness is the first thing to drive the action in 1 Samuel, and that by itself is quite significant coming after the book of Judges. In Judges, many women are victims of circumstances far beyond their control, and their pain is never vindicated. If Hannah's story were told in the book of Judges, we'd likely wince the second she was introduced because few women make it out of Judges unscathed, let alone alive. But Hannah's story will immediately play out much differently. Here, she will suffer, but her suffering is only a prelude to God's decisive action on her behalf. By the end of 1 Samuel, not only will Hannah's pain be vindicated, but the grace given to Hannah will turn out to rule the fate of Israel and Judah.

Rather than trying to beat her rival wife by using an enslaved woman to bear her a child, as Rachel and Leah did, Hannah decides to take her childlessness into her own hands and swears an oath to God that she will dedicate a male child to God's lifelong service if only she is allowed to conceive (1:11). Hannah's prayer is a success: She conceives and gives birth (1:20). Samuel is then dedicated to God's service, retroactively making good on Elkanah's name, which means "God has acquired," as in, God has acquired a servant through Elkanah.

Hannah is said to celebrate the dedication of Samuel to God's service with another prayer (2:1–10). This prayer, however, was almost certainly composed by some other author for some other occasion and then inserted here.[1] A casual reading of the prayer reveals that it has little to do with Hannah's specific situation. Only the second half of v. 5 speaks about overcoming childlessness, and those lines look to be an editorial addition that interrupts the poetic structure of the prayer. The prayer also anachronistically looks forward to a king (2:10) long before the possibility of a king is raised in the story.

Still, the prayer is kinda fun to read where it is. We can imagine Hannah boasting over her enemies (2:1), that is, Peninnah. We can imagine Hannah indirectly and cleverly chiding Eli for his misunderstanding of her prayer for a child (2:3). We can celebrate Hannah's affirmation of her own faithfulness (2:9a) and turn up our noses at Peninnah and Eli when Hannah calls them wicked by proxy (2:9b).

The rest of Hannah's prayer celebrates the reversal of the fortunes of the privileged (2:4–8). In that way, it's similar to Mary's famous prayer in Luke 1, the Magnificat, which also celebrates the humbling of the proud and the lifting up of the lowly (Luke 1:52–53).

Hannah then disappears from the story after we're told that she goes on to have several more children (2:21). Her short time in 1 Samuel is quite remarkable. Not only do the consequences of her prayer reverberate throughout the rest of the Bible, but she is one of the only significant characters in 1 and 2 Samuel who gets what they want. The rest of 1 and 2 Samuel are filled with stories of powerful warriors and conquering heroes; but in the end, Hannah alone claims a flawless victory for herself.

Eli

Eli, whose name means "to ascend," is introduced as a priest with a prestigious post, sitting near the entrance to the sanctuary where the ark of the covenant was kept (1:9). But no sooner is he introduced

---

[1] I wish I could tell you who that other author is. So far as I know, no one knows. But given the prayer's national scope, emphasis on military victory, and presumption of a king, it was probably composed by a priest well into the monarchical period to celebrate Israel's victory over an enemy.

than he misjudges Hannah's silent prayer, thinking she's drunk and mumbling to herself (1:12–14). First impressions matter, both in life and in biblical narrative, and the first thing a character says in 1 and 2 Samuel is often representative of who they are. Based on this standard, Eli comes off as a bad judge of character and someone who doesn't recognize genuine piety when he sees it. This turns out to be painfully accurate.

Apart from exchanging some perfunctory conversation with Hannah, Eli is next described as having corrupt sons (2:12–17). For context, it was common in ancient Israel for animal sacrifices to involve setting some portions of the sacrificed animal aside for God, some for the priest presiding over the sacrifice, and some for the one offering the sacrifice. Eli's sons insist on eating the portion set aside for God (2:15) and threaten violence if anyone tries to do it properly (2:16). Later, we're told they sleep with women serving at the sanctuary (2:22), which is almost certainly coercive. Eli's plaintive attempts to rebuke his sons fail (2:23–25), and in a lengthy monologue (2:27–36) an anonymous man of God condemns Eli's sons and future descendants to violent deaths.

At the risk of stating the obvious, Eli is a bad father. What we see in 1 Samuel 2 is the culmination of a lifetime of Eli's failures to instill even basic moral values in his sons, all while he benefited from the privilege their tyranny over the sanctuary brought. Eli's lack of response to his condemnation, and his nonchalant response to Samuel repeating the condemnation in 3:18, admits neither responsibility nor remorse. There are several characters in 1 and 2 Samuel about which it's probably appropriate to feel conflicted even in the face of the terrible things they've done. I don't think Eli is one of them. Feel free to just hate him.

The condemnation of Eli in 1 Samuel 2 is a theologically dense statement. Three features are worth noting. We're told that God had previously promised Eli that his family would minister before God forever (2:30), but the Bible nowhere records such a promise, and such a promise seems unwise in retrospect. This won't be the last time in 1 and 2 Samuel where God makes a forever promise to a person only to go back on it later. Keep that in mind.

A second feature worth noting is God's assertion that he will raise up a faithful priest to replace Eli and his descendants (2:35). This priest is, of course, Samuel, and we're told that one of his jobs will be to minister before "God's anointed," which is another reference to a future king.

I should pause for just a second here to point out that this verse is why this section is titled "Samuel vs. Eli." Samuel's rise to prominence doesn't occur in a vacuum. It's inexorably tied to the fall of Eli. This kind of narrative conflict is a common feature in 1 and 2 Samuel. One person's ambitious gain is another person's tragic loss.

Perhaps most surprisingly, God appears content to operate within this kind of narrative conflict, championing the cause of one character against another whom God had previously championed only a moment before. This makes God look as fickle and as opportunistic as the human characters God is sovereign over. But frankly, this is the way God can easily appear in the face of quickly shifting political fortunes. The text is honest about the way it feels to try to discern God's role in history.

The third and final feature of Eli's condemnation worth noting, at least to tuck away in the back of our minds, is how total the decimation of Eli's house is promised to be. God doesn't just commit to punishing Eli's sons; God commits to punishing every member of Eli's house in perpetuity. We'll refer back to punishment on several occasions, as it will claim the lives of many characters throughout 1 and 2 Samuel.

God

A quick note about God, given that first impressions matter. God has many names and titles in the Bible, but the first we see in 1 Samuel 1 is in verse 3. We're told that, year after year, Elkanah goes to Shiloh to sacrifice to "Yahweh Tzevaot," which you'll probably see translated in your English Bible as either God Almighty or LORD of Hosts. The second of these is more linguistically accurate but it might not mean much to you, especially if you ever had a job as a restaurant host/hostess and you're wondering why God is going to show you to your seat.

"Yahweh" is the god of Israel's personal name, and there is a famous story involving a burning (but not actually burning) bush in Exodus 3, where God shares the name with Moses. Biblical scholars don't agree on what "Yahweh" means or exactly where it comes from, but it seems to be related to the idea of "being." Because of the Jewish taboo on saying God's personal name, various substitutes have been used and "Lord" is one of the most common.

Tzevaot are "hosts." The hosts that Yahweh is lord of are armies, both of the divine/angelic kind and the more conventional human kind. Since this is the first name and title of God we encounter in these stories, it sets the mood for what kind of god we're dealing with. God is going to be a god of military action in these stories, directly influencing the outcome of battles and taking sides when people go to war.

That can be troubling for people who are new to reading the Bible or who're expecting a god like gentle Jesus meek and mild. But we should keep in mind that God is often whatever biblical authors need God to be, and that prompts us to ask the following question: what kind of circumstances must these biblical authors be writing in to need a god like this? A person who needs a god to control war is a person afraid of war, and there's hardly been a point in ancient Israelite history where Israel wasn't surrounded by stronger empires. If we're sitting in more comfortable circumstances today, we might find a god of war distasteful; but perhaps a god of war might also make us more sympathetic to the biblical authors.

Samuel

Hannah names her first born son Samuel—a play on the Hebrew phrase "God has heard," as in, God heard her prayer. The miraculous circumstances surrounding Samuel's birth are similar to those of Samson, whose mother was also childless until divine intervention (Judges 13).

But Samuel's first encounter with God in 1 Samuel 3 is more reminiscent of the auditory experience of the prophet Jeremiah, who received the "word of the LORD" when he was called to be a prophet (Jeremiah 1). That's fitting, since Samuel himself is a figure of transition, half from the world of Judges before and half from the world of kings and prophets that will come after.

Samuel is raised, for better or worse, with Eli at the sanctuary in Shiloh. That means he would have grown up as a witness to the abuses of Eli's house; and Eli, who calls Samuel "my son" (1 Samuel 3:16), would have been more a father to him than Elkanah ever was. It must have been quite disturbing for Samuel, still a child, that his first encounter with God culminates in God's declaration that the house of Eli is coming to an end (3:11–14). Indeed, the first emotion described of Samuel is his fear (3:15) at the prospect of telling Eli what God has revealed to him. Again, first impressions matter, and Samuel's are awash in confusion and fear as he mistakes the sound of his divine father for his adopted human father (3:4).

Regardless of Samuel's fearful introduction to God's service, Samuel grows into a famous prophet, known throughout Israel from Dan to Beersheba (3:20), which serve as the classical markers for the most northern and most southern points in the country, respectively. The word of God is continually revealed to Samuel at Shiloh, not in the form of a written text but in visions (3:1, 21).

With Samuel's prophetic career established, the introduction to 1 Samuel is complete. The story so far has given us the expectation that Eli's end will be just around the corner and that Samuel will be significant because of his role as a kingmaker.

Let's see what happens next.

The Ark vs. the Philistines (1 Samuel 4–7)

The story turns away from Samuel and his burgeoning prophetic career for several chapters to describe a war between the Israelites and the

Philistines. Israel's army brings the ark of the covenant with them into battle as a symbol of God's presence; but rather than securing their victory over the Philistines, the ark proves ineffective. The Philistines rally, Israel is defeated, and the ark is captured.

The Philistines bring the ark of the covenant back to their capital temple to lay in defeat before statues of their deities. But the ark itself miraculously resists, and in a series of supernatural escapades, it manages to return itself back to Israelite hands.

Samuel then reappears, and after offering a sacrifice on behalf of the Israelites, the Philistine armies are devastated by divine intervention and Israel wins the day.

The Ark

The ark of the covenant is a wooden chest covered in gold and decorated with cherubim—monstrous divine beings that guard sacred spaces. Detailed instructions for the construction of the ark are given by God in Exodus 37:1–9, but it's possible that these stories in 1 Samuel are older and unaware of those texts.[2] The ark was said to hold the tablets of the Ten Commandments, but its primary function was like that of an Egyptian bark, a cultic vessel used to transport the special presence of a deity during religious processions. The ark led the people of Israel through their wilderness wandering, across the Red Sea, across the Jordan River, and in their alleged battles to conquer Canaan. The expectation given in Numbers 10:35 was that, if the ark was brought to battle, God would scatter Israel's enemies.

That's the expectation that likely influenced the Israelites in 1 Samuel 4. Following a defeat at the hands of the Philistines (4:1–2), the Israelites decided to bring the ark with them into battle, along with Eli's sons, Hophni and Phinehas (4:3–4). If you've been paying

---

[2] The way the Bible came together is complex. The order books appear is rarely related to the order they were written in.

attention, you know there's only one way this can go at this point. Despite the ark initially raising Israelite morale (4:5–6), the Philistines manage to fight through their fear, utterly destroy the Israelite army, and capture the ark of the covenant (4:7–11). Hophni and Phinehas are killed in battle, becoming the first casualties of God's condemnation of Eli's house.

In an extended scene paced for dramatic effect, Eli hears of the death of his sons and the capture of the ark, at which point he falls over and dies (4:18). The narrator informs us that Eli had judged Israel for forty years, which is the common formula in the book of Judges to denote the end of a judge's career. Though Eli never appears on a list of judges and never leads anyone into battle like an actual judge, the text seems willing to accord him that final honor.

Back to the box. The Philistines are now in possession of the ark of the covenant. Ancient West Asian (AWA)[3] cultures practiced "godnapping," the stealing of the idols and other religious iconography of defeated peoples. Such stolen goods were brought to a victor's temple to be displayed in subjugation before statues representing the victor's deities. Since ancient people often believed that their deities determined the outcome of battles, this was an appropriate end for a conflict, with representations of a defeated party's gods bowing before the victorious party's gods.

It's with this practice in mind that the Philistines take the ark of the covenant to their city of Ashdod and put the ark before a statue of their head deity, Dagon (5:1–2). In any other situation, that's where the story would end. But lo and behold, the ark doesn't take its captivity lying down, and it knocks over the statue of Dagon (5:3), cuts off its hands and head (5:4), afflicts the Philistines with tumors (5:6), and then begins to indiscriminately kill people as it's shuffled from one Philistine city to the next (5:7–12). Eventually, the Philistines put the ark in a wagon, and the wagon drives itself back to Israelite lands (6:10–12).

---

[3] Also known as the Ancient Near East.

Unfortunately, the ark is not done taking lives, and 1 Samuel 6:19–7:2 relates a strange anecdote about how the ark kills seventy people in the Israelite village of Beth-shemesh and then needs to be relocated to the nearby Kiriath-Jearim.

This might be a good opportunity to explain that the ancient Israelites thought of the presence of their deity as something powerful and dangerous, not unlike a nuclear reactor. Nuclear reactors can be safe if the proper ritual precautions and safeguards are in place, but even the slightest slip-up could lead to lethal accidents. In this way, God's presence was sometimes thought of less like the presence of a person, who might choose to lash out in this or that way, and more like the presence of an impersonal force that will harm anyone who is improperly exposed to it. This is why the instructions for constructing the tabernacle, which was believed to house God's presence, and for maintaining the ritual purity of everyone who interacts with it is taken so seriously in the books of Exodus and Numbers.[4] They are attempting to bottle lightning. That might not make us feel any better about the lives the ark casually takes, but at least it makes some sense of why the biblical authors would tell a story like this.

The ark stays in Kiriath-Jearim for the remainder of 1 Samuel, and we do not hear about it again for some time.

The Philistines

In 1 Samuel 4, we are introduced to the Philistines, a people who were recurring villains in ancient Israel's history. The Philistines were a foreign ethnic group who had only recently come to Canaan, likely from Greek islands during the 12th century BCE as part of that same late Bronze Age collapse that disrupted so many other nations in the region. They were culturally and technologically sophisticated, despite the

---

[4] The instructions for building the tabernacle begin in Exodus 25, continue to 31, are interrupted by the story of the golden calf (Exodus 32–34), then resume through the end of the book. The tabernacle is completed in Numbers 7 and God's presence takes up residence in Numbers 9:15–23.

negative connotation that the term "Philistine" can have, and in time they came to use a Canaanite dialect for their language, which made communication between Philistines and Israelites easy. Philistines are mocked by Israelite characters as "uncircumcised," a pretty juvenile insult, owing to the fact that the Philistines didn't practice circumcision as the Egyptians and Canaanites did. Dagon was adopted as the national god of the Philistines, a patriarchal god of prosperity who had been worshiped throughout Mesopotamia for centuries before the Philistines arrived.

The Philistines primarily settled in five city-states along the coast of southwestern Canaan. The contemporary term "Palestine" ultimately derives from the Hebrew and Egyptian words for "Philistine." There is no ethnic relation between the ancient Philistines, who ceased to exist by the 5th century BCE, and later Palestinians, though Gaza was one of the Philistine city-states

The Philistines in 1 Samuel 4 exhibit strange beliefs about the Israelites. When the Philistines get word that the ark has come to the battle, they cry out for someone to save them from the "mighty gods who plagued Egypt in the wilderness" (4:6–8). For some reason, the Philistines thought the Israelites were polytheistic and that it was the Egyptians who suffered plagues in the wilderness rather than the Israelites themselves. Odd. The biblical author seems to be making fun of the Philistines, by imagining their misunderstanding of Israelite religion and history. But later, when the Philistines are debating what to do with the ark, their priests have a detailed knowledge of the Exodus story where Pharaoh hardened his heart (6:6).

Pretending adversarial cultures care about your stories is kind of cringe, and it's a good reminder that we're not reading about the Philistines from a Philistine point of view. The Philistines themselves left behind little writing. These stories in 1 and 2 Samuel aren't an unbiased documentary on Philistine culture. They're polemical texts, written by biased Israelite authors with limited knowledge of the subject for the express purpose of affirming their superiority over the Philistines.

Despite the bias against the Philistines, they're smart enough to eventually figure out a magical cure for the havoc caused by the captured ark of the covenant (6:7–9) and successfully send it away. The Philistines then remain a staple feature of 1 and 2 Samuel until the bitter end.

Samuel

Samuel reappears in 1 Samuel 7, and here he is in full judge-mode. Though we haven't been told recently that the Israelites had begun to worship other gods, we are told that they turned back to worshiping God (7:2), and Samuel leads them in a ritual of purification (7:3–4). The trope of the Israelites worshiping other gods, getting beat up by other groups, and then turning back to God is the defining trope of the book of Judges, and the remainder of 1 Samuel 7 could easily have been an appendix to that earlier book.

The Philistines assemble to fight Israel again (7:7), but Samuel invites God's intervention with a sacrifice (7:9), and God defeats the Philistines with thunder (7:10). This highly idealized and theological view of battle, where human actors are all but unnecessary and God does all the work, is reminiscent of the battle of Jericho in Joshua 6. This view is actually rare in 1 and 2 Samuel, where it's more common for God to give human warriors success rather than to fight battles on their behalf.

When Samuel and/or God defeats the Philistines, the narrator informs us that the Philistines didn't enter Israelite territory again for the rest of Samuel's life (7:13). This turns out to be false, repeatedly, and a weird mistake for the narrator to make. Unless, of course, the narrator didn't make a mistake, and, in an earlier version of this story, this was the end. It certainly seems like *an* end, as Samuel is given the formulaic Judges sign-off (7:15) like Eli before him, signaling the completion of his career. This sign-off invites us to imagine a simpler version of Samuel's life, where his whole story involved revealing the downfall of Eli's house and then defeating the Philistines after the return of the ark.

In this simpler, hypothetical version of the story, there are no kings on the horizon, and Israel exists permanently in the cycle of sin, obedience, and deliverance that typifies the book of Judges. It's almost sweet in its simplicity, but later versions of this story can't be put off forever. As I said in the introduction, authors kept coming back to these stories to add to them and find new meaning in them. Like the retired protagonist at the beginning of some action-thriller, just when Samuel thought he was out, events will pull him back in.

Samuel vs. Israel (1 Samuel 8)

A group of elders abruptly confront Samuel and demand to have a king appointed over them. Samuel is hostile to the idea and confers with God, who expresses sadness but relents. Samuel warns the elders that a king will be an oppressive figure and that God won't save them from this oppression, but the elders disregard the warning and demand a king regardless. Samuel dismisses the elders and sets out to find a king.

Samuel

The scene in 1 Samuel 8 is a watershed moment, standing on the border between the judges who came before and the kings who will come after. In the form of the story that we have today, the preceding war with the Philistines and the Israelites' desperate dependence on Samuel and God for their protection seem to be the motivation for the elders' demand for a king. Here, a king represents a more conventional and more stable way of defending the people from military threats. Charismatic judges are cool and all, but they're not very reliable, especially in their personal lives. And it's this concern about the personal life of a judge that brings the elders to Samuel.

A lifetime must have passed since 1 Samuel 3 before the ark's capture, because, in the first verses of 1 Samuel 8, we're told that Samuel has grown old, that he has sons, and that they are corrupt (8:1–3). The ghost of Eli rears its head. As I pointed out before, Samuel was much more a son of Eli than of Elkanah, and it seems that Samuel inherited Eli's weaknesses as a man and as a father. Samuel's sons Joel and Abijah take bribes. In a world where independent regional leaders were the sole means of jurisprudence and where eyewitness testimony was the best evidence people could hope for, there was effectively no law when officials took bribes.

In some ways Samuel is worse than Eli. With Eli, we at least got a half-hearted attempt on his part to rebuke his sons; but with Samuel we get nothing. He never addresses the evil of his sons in narration. He never even recognizes it. We might wonder what Samuel has been doing in the time between 1 Samuel 3 and 8 in order to model this unjust behavior for his sons. Perhaps he was as absent from their lives as he was from the narration. The one narrative detail we get in support of this absentee father hypothesis comes from 1 Samuel 7:16, which reports that Samuel traveled throughout Israel year after year in his capacity as a judge. And while he did come home to Ramah to hold court (7:17), his sons served in Beersheba, more than fifty miles south of Samuel's travels. While the text does not explicitly say so, this seems like an indictment to me. Samuel was a career man, infatuated with his own fame, and he had no time for his sons.

The corruption of Samuel's sons is public knowledge, as the elders state it as the immediate motivation for their desire for a king. Perhaps in another world, where Eli had been a better father to Samuel and Samuel had been a better father to Joel and Abijah, the prophet would have righteous sons who could serve as his successors. But alas, it's not so, and the elders step in to secure a future for themselves.

God

God has been active in the story thus far, allowing Hannah to conceive, condemning Eli's household, raising up Samuel to fame, afflicting and killing random people in proximity to the ark, and defeating the Philistines. But 1 Samuel 8 features a more thoughtful deity for the first time. When the elders ask Samuel for a king and Samuel consults God, God utters one of the most grief-stricken lines in biblical narrative: "It's not you they've rejected, but me" (8:7).

The theological ideal from Judges was that God was king. That's why, when Gideon is asked by his people to rule over them in Judges 8:23, he declines and says God is their ruler. It's also why, toward the end of Judges when things are at their darkest, the narrator repeats the refrain, "In those days there was no king, and everyone did what was right in their own eyes" (Judges 17:6; 21:25). The refrain probably doesn't bemoan the lack of a human king but rather the lack of popular recognition that God is king. So when the elders in 1 Samuel 8 ask for a king, in the mind of the author they are asking for a replacement for God, hence God's grief-stricken response.[5]

Nevertheless, God is in a deferential mood and allows the elders to have a king so long as Samuel warns them about how terrible a king will be (8:9). It's a testament to the elders' dissatisfaction with the current state of affairs that, even after hearing how a king will oppress them, they choose to have one regardless. Their commitment to replacing God is sincere and not without merit. The cycle of Judges doesn't seem to be good for anyone, least of all the powerless. If that's the best that God's kingship can afford, you can understand the people's desire for something, perhaps anything, else.

God's attitude toward a king in 1 Samuel 8 makes answering the question "Does God actually want a king over Israel?" an exercise in ambivalence. The answer can't possibly be a straightforward "yes." It's clearly not God's first or even second choice. If a person agrees to

---

[5] When I showed someone an earlier version of this chapter, she said that this scenario sounds like a reversal of the freedom the Israelites attained in the exodus stories. They left an oppressive foreign ruler only to arrive in the promised land and, rather than serving God, opted to serve an oppressive leader chosen from among their own people. I agree, this does in fact sound like that, and that's sad :(

something only out of great disappointment, are they really endorsing it? From this point on, we'll begin to see biblical authors with a more positive view of the monarchy. Many of them will go out of their way to craft a theology where God enthusiastically and permanently endorses the monarchy; and these earlier passages, where God is only begrudgingly on board, will be forgotten.

Another thing God almost does in 1 Samuel 8 is set new hypothetical terms by which the people's relationship with God will function. During the time of the Judges, the Israelites would cry out to God for a savior, and God would eventually send them one, even if it was one of questionable character. But through Samuel, God relays that, when the Israelites cry out to God for a savior to deliver them from their oppressive king, God won't help at all. They'll be on their own. These terms, however, are more like when a tired parent announces a more severe punishment than they're willing to follow through on and then ends up doing something less severe when their child disobeys. God does in fact continue to help the Israelites even when they cry out because of an oppressive king.

One of the most substantial changes 1 Samuel 8 heralds isn't said out loud, but it radically alters both the narrative and the theology that follows. Prior to 1 Samuel 8, whichever character had special access to God or was empowered by God's spirit was also the national leader. Moses, Joshua, and all the judges who followed were this way, combining religious and civil leadership in a single person. But once Samuel sets out to find a king, an irrevocable divide forms between these two kinds of leadership, and no one person will hold both again.

Kings will take up civil leadership, beginning with Saul who will be in charge of the military and administration. But then a prophet, like Samuel himself at the beginning, will hold power as a religious leader. This pattern continues throughout both 1 and 2 Samuel and 1 and 2 Kings.

For sure, the king's power does have a religious dimension, but he remains open to a kind of checks and balances by a prophetic figure whose criticisms ostensibly come from God. Samuel will criticize Saul;

Nathan will criticize David; Ahijah will criticize Solomon; Elijah will criticize Ahab, etc., etc. The relationship between king and prophet is rarely agreeable, and so the relationship between the king and God is often complex as well. The hostilities between kings, prophets, and the god behind them will drive many stories going forward.

The Elders

Samuel becomes the mouthpiece in chapter 8 for some rather pronounced anti-monarchical sentiments, listing at length all the ways kings will overly tax, enslave, and otherwise mistreat their own people out of greed or pursuit of more power (8:10–17). If you remember from the introduction, 1 and 2 Samuel have both an anti-monarchical voice and a pro-monarchical voice, but we've yet to see the latter. Both chapters 7 and 8 are resoundingly opposed to having a king. God's direct victory over the Philistines in chapter 7 makes a king superfluous, and the long list in chapter 8 of malicious practices kings will commit makes a king undesirable.

It should be noted that neither Saul nor David, the first two kings of Israel, are especially guilty of these practices. For all their plentiful faults, economic exploitation isn't really among them. These practices are, however, much more descriptive of the third king of Israel, Solomon, David's son. Samuel's list here seems to be looking forward several generations to Solomon's rule, which is economically extravagant and does involve the enslavement of his own people.

Although the narrator casts these anti-monarchical sentiments in Samuel's voice, they're much more reflective of the perspective of the elders, if such elders actually existed. Samuel himself doesn't really stand to be affected one way or the other by the existence of a king, apart from having to stand aside for someone else to be in charge. The elders, on the other hand, and the common people they represent are the ones who will be hurt most by an oppressive king. It's their food and animals that will be taken, their money that will be taxed, and their sons and daughters who will be forced into servitude.

While it's highly unlikely that this story is historical, the concerns it reflects are realistic. Reconfiguring society with a king, with all the centralization, bureaucracy, and taxation that entails, would be a concerning change however it happened. Power would be taken from regional elders and concentrated in the hands of a single man without much accountability. As a result, it's probable that this chapter was written by some scribe, generations after Samuel's time, who was living in the midst of the worst abuses of a king and who decided to retroactively place their own complaints in Samuel's more authoritative mouth. "Look here," the scribe could then say, "we should have known this was going to turn out bad."

One of the most provocative lines placed in the mouth of the elders in chapter 8 is repeated in verses 5 and 20. Part of their motivation for wanting a king, they say, is "so we will be like other peoples." This isn't necessarily the actual view of the elders, but it's the view opposed to the narrator's own, and the elders are a convenient mouthpiece for it. The narrator strongly believes that God is the sole, proper king of Israel; to have a human king would therefore destroy the cultural uniqueness of ancient Israelite society. To have a king is to trade away what makes the Israelites *Israelites*—a kingdom of priests (Exodus 19:6), chosen from all the peoples of the earth and held to unique standards (Amos 3:2). The earliest laws in the Bible in Exodus 20–23 never mention a king; rather, it's the priesthood, the prophets, and the special access to God that's definitive of Israelite identity. Since we know where the story is going and since we know that eventually biblical authors will develop theology supportive of a king, it's difficult for this moment in the narrative to hit with full force. But try to imagine for just a moment what it would be like to have everything you thought made your people *your people* destroyed overnight. It would cause a crippling existential crisis, and the ghost of that crisis haunts 1 Samuel 8.

Though it's likely no consolation to the author of 1 Samuel 8, the mood has already changed by the time we turn the page to 1 Samuel 9, and we're on our way to find the first king of Israel.

Saul vs. the Editor (1 Samuel 9–12)

In 1 Samuel 9–11, Saul will be chosen to be the king of Israel in three separate stories. First, Samuel will be directed to Saul by a series of miraculous coincidences, and Samuel will anoint him in a private ceremony. Second, Saul will be publicly chosen to be king by lot. Third, a foreign enemy will threaten Israel, and as with the judges of ages past, the spirit of God will come over Saul, and he will then defeat the enemy in battle. Following his victory, Saul will be declared king by the people through charismatic consensus.

With a king chosen, Samuel gives a farewell speech, where he exonerates himself of any wrongdoing during his time as a leader. He then echoes the theology of 1 Samuel 8, decrying the choice to have a king and even threatening the people with destruction if they don't obey God.

Saul

In 1 Samuel 9, we are introduced to Saul, whose name means "asked for." There have been several puns earlier in 1 Samuel that have played on Saul's name (1:17, 20, 27; 8:10), foreshadowing his eventual arrival. We're immediately told that Saul is handsome, tall, and the son of a wealthy man (9:1–2), exactly the kind of guy you or God would swipe right on.[6]

Our first impression of Saul is ambiguous. He enters the scene searching for his father's lost donkeys (9:3). Donkeys can be a symbol of royalty, so this image of Saul chasing after them implies he's an ambitious character who desires the throne. But his first line of dialogue is to express a desire to give up and go home in case his father is worried about him (9:5). This seems to undermine any ambition implied by the opening image, and we're left wondering whether Saul really wants

---

[6] I see the way you're looking at him.

the throne or not. We'll continue to wonder for the remainder of both the book and his reign.

I can't help but point out how Saul's dialogue implies something about his relationship with his father. The word "to worry" in verse 5 is rare in biblical Hebrew, appearing only seven times in the whole Hebrew Bible.[7] It's also rare that we're told about a son guessing his father's emotions. Saul's suspicion that his father will stop caring about the donkeys and start worrying about him turns out to be true (10:2). This might not seem like a lot, but frankly, it's one of the few examples of men's emotional intelligence anywhere in biblical narrative.[8] It also implies that Saul knows his father well, and conversely, that Saul's father cares about him more than he does the donkeys and the wealth they represent. This reciprocation, and the relationship that must exist behind this reciprocation, is a positive example of fatherhood. A child can only accurately predict a parent's emotions in a healthy way if the parent has made a habit of openly disclosing their emotions to their child. This requires transparency, and transparency requires vulnerability. While it would be unwise to overly romanticize Saul's father, these virtues are worth recognizing and practicing in our own lives.

As mentioned in the outline earlier, what follows are three different stories of Saul becoming king, none of which seem to be aware of the others, and the second and third stories are totally redundant. This kind of conflicting redundancy is the marker of literary doublets, which are often used by biblical scholars to parse out multiple authors behind a text. The literary doublets in the Pentateuch are the most familiar. There are two creation stories (Genesis 1:1–2:3 vs. Genesis 2:4–25) and two flood stories that have been interwoven between Genesis 6–9 with two different numbers of animals to bring on the ark (Genesis 6:19–20 vs. Genesis 7:2–3), two different lengths of the flood (Genesis

---

[7] In case you're curious, you can find the other instances in 1 Samuel 10:2, Psalm 38:18, Isaiah 57:11, Jeremiah 17:8, 38:19, and 42:16. Apparently people didn't worry much back then. Love that for them.

[8] Anywhere in the world, tbh.

7:4 vs. Genesis 7:24), and two promises from God not to do it again (Genesis 8:21 vs. Genesis 9:11). There are also two stories of Abraham's covenant with God (Genesis 15 vs. Genesis 17), three sister-wife stories (Genesis 12 vs. Genesis 20 vs. Genesis 26), two stories of the revelation of the divine name to Moses (Exodus 3 vs. Exodus 6), and dozens more. In 1 and 2 Samuel, we have more heavily edited doublets, but they're there regardless, and the repetition of Saul becoming king is pretty easy to see.

In the first story of Saul becoming king, Saul bumps into Samuel, who has been told by God that Saul is to be king. Saul's pursuit of his father's lost donkeys takes him throughout central Israel on a course not unlike the one Samuel used to travel (9:4). But when Saul doesn't have any luck finding the donkeys, the servant traveling with him suggests going to a nearby town to see an anonymous seer (9:5), who is later identified as Samuel. Some biblical scholars have speculated that, in an earlier version of this story, Samuel wasn't involved at all, just some generic man of God. The edited version of the story we have today includes Samuel to make it fit with the surrounding material.

When Saul arrives at Samuel's place, Samuel tells him that his donkeys have been found (9:20). Then, they eat together (9:22–24), and Samuel anoints[9] Saul as king (10:1). In ancient Israel, anointing was a sign of setting something apart for a special task; most conventionally, priests and kings were anointed. For his part, Saul receives Samuel's attention with humility (9:21), and Saul says that he is unworthy to be chosen by God like Moses (Exodus 3:11) and Gideon (Judges 6:15). Samuel then describes to Saul a series of signs that he will experience when he leaves, which will act as confirmation that Samuel's anointing is legitimate (10:2–8). The last of these signs—to wait seven days at Gilgal for Samuel to arrive before offering a sacrifice (10:8)—will come back to haunt Saul years later in a rather strange way.

We're told that Saul experiences all of the signs Samuel said he would and that God gives him another heart (10:9), which is a poetic

---

[9] Lol essential oils.

way of saying that God has caused a change of character in Saul which makes him fit for his new purpose. The first evidence of this change, apparently, is to fall into an ecstatic trance with a band of prophets (10:10).

This story of Saul becoming king closes with an editorial comment that Saul did not tell his family, or presumably anyone else, about being made king (10:16). This comment helps explain the redundant stories of Saul becoming king that follows and almost certainly wasn't original to the story. Even if Saul himself didn't tell anyone, it's unlikely that Samuel wouldn't, since the entire point of having a king was to satisfy the request of the elders from 1 Samuel 8.

If God gave Saul a new heart fit for his anointed role, the second story of Saul becoming king doesn't know it. In 1 Samuel 10:17–24, Samuel gathers the people of Israel together by tribes, then he casts lots to determine who will be king. We're not exactly sure what this practice involved—whether short sticks, marked stones, or something like dice—but whatever it was, it was used as a form of divination to answer simple questions at God's direction. Here, the use of lots picks out a tribe, then a family, and then a person to be king. Guess what? It's Saul (10:21). Saul, though, was hiding among the supply wagons (10:22) that would no doubt accompany a large gathering like this. This doesn't look like a man who has a new heart, or really any heart at all, and it's only when he's dragged in front of the gathered people and they again notice his height[10] that he's proclaimed king (10:24). Mission successful, I guess.

The third and final story of Saul becoming king is narrated in chapter 11, and it is the most straightforward of the stories. Some villainous character named Nahash the Ammonite is gallivanting around, gouging out people's eyes (11:1–2). When Saul hears about this, the spirit of God comes upon him (11:6) like the judges of yesteryear. Saul chops up a couple of oxen and sends the pieces off to the tribes of Israel (11:7). Dismemberment was a common penalty for breaking an

---

[10] How many red flags would you ignore because he's tall?

ancient covenant, so Saul's basically saying, "If you don't show up to fight these guys, I'm gonna chop you up too."

It works, and the text says 330,000 people show up to fight Nahash (11:8). This number is silly, higher than reasonable population estimates of the entire land of Israel during this time. With his giant army, Saul annihilates Nahash and his forces (11:11). The people who are following him are so impressed that they offer to execute anyone who doubted Saul before (11:12). But Saul doesn't want those vibes (11:13), so they go to Gilgal where Saul is made king by popular acclaim, and they have a big party (11:14–15).[11]

The narrative in 1 Samuel 11 is one of the most pro-monarchical passages in the book. Unlike 1 Samuel 7, where a king is entirely superfluous because Samuel can just offer a sacrifice and God will blow up Israel's enemies with thunder, here a king is presented as necessary for the defense of the kingdom. The spirit of God not only empowers Saul but acts as a marker of divine legitimacy. God is saying yes to the dress, where the dress in question is Saul's ability to successfully lead an army of ridiculous size and kick Nahash's ass all over the place. When Saul is made king, the text goes out of its way to say it takes place in the presence of God, again, a marker of divine legitimacy. If you just read 1 Samuel 11, you'd be forced to conclude that God is a big fan of Israel having a king as none of the former skepticism is evident here. It's probably not a coincidence that the lack of skepticism correlates with the lack of Samuel, who isn't present in the story.[12]

The reason this section is titled "Saul vs. the Editor" is because, after these three redundant stories, we don't really have a good sense of who Saul is. He is young and sensitive in chapter 9, cowardly in chapter 10, and fearsome in chapter 11. Whoever edited these stories together clearly had an interest in preserving a range of material they had access to, but they didn't seem to care about whether or not the

---

[11] As one does.

[12] Samuel is mentioned in a name-droppy fashion at the end of 11:7, but this is probably added later and doesn't amount to much anyway.

final product gave us a coherent characterization of Saul. The editor has barely tried to connect the stories, and Saul more than anyone else suffers from it. That's unfortunate, because after 1 Samuel 11, it's all downhill for Saul, and it would be nice to have had a clear picture of the man who will be doomed to failure in the chapters that follow.

Samuel

Samuel returns in chapter 12 after not doing much in chapters 9–11. If chapter 11 was one of the most pro-monarchical chapters we've had so far, chapter 12 is the most anti-monarchical. Cast as Samuel's farewell address, chapter 12 is essentially a long rant about how stupid and evil the Israelites are for wanting a king and how dead the king is going to be if he messes up. As a farewell address it's ironic, since Samuel remains active in the narrative for another four chapters without slowing down, and he doesn't actually die until 1 Samuel 25:1. If anything, Samuel's most decisive scenes haven't even happened yet, and that makes him look like a man who's having trouble turning things over to the next generation.

Samuel begins his speech by saying he's old, and his sons are with the people (12:2). Given the moral quality of his sons, this is probably more awkward than anything. Samuel then says he's dealt honestly with the people in his capacity as leader, in contrast to the alleged practices of a king (12:3–5). This is a strange claim, since he has just mentioned his sons who are famous for being unjust. I don't know how much credit you get for being honest when you bring your bribery-accepting sons with you.

In 1 Samuel 12:6–11, we are given a historical review, where Samuel rehearses some of the major moments in Israelite history. When we get to verse 12, things shift gears. Samuel explains that the people wanted a king because of the threat posed by Nahash the Ammonite. This is a strange line, since the elders approached Samuel about a king several chapters before Nahash was introduced. Back then, it was the threat of the Philistines that seemed to prompt the elders to want a king. Verse

12 thinks no one asked for a king until Nahash, and no one does ask for a king when Nahash is a threat in chapter 11. This narrative discontinuity is likely another example of older stories being edited together into their current form. Chapter 12 is really going out of its way to talk crap about chapter 11, probably because of how positive it was about the monarchy.

The rest of chapter 12 repeats a theology of retribution several times (12:14–15, 24–25), where, if the Israelites and their king obey God, things will be fine, but if the Israelites or their king disobey God, terrible things will happen to them. This is a big part of the theology that Israel used after the Babylonian exile in the 6th century BCE to make sense of why they were so thoroughly defeated. Generally, if a nation was defeated in the ancient world, it was believed that the nation's god had been defeated by another god. But the biblical authors couldn't tolerate this conventional explanation, so they came up with this idea that God had agreed to support the monarchy only if the king obeyed. If the king didn't, though, God would destroy the people of Israel. This allowed later Israelite authors to say their defeat by Babylon wasn't a defeat of Yahweh at all; rather, it was Yahweh's will. In other words, God wanted the Israelites to be defeated because of their disobedience. This shifts the blame away from God and toward the people, and while that might seem like an uncomfortable trade to make, it was ultimately successful in allowing the Israelites to endure Babylonian captivity with their religious identity intact.[13] If this was the editor's goal, they achieved it.

As if to dispel any possible doubt about how Samuel feels about the whole king situation, Samuel declares that asking for a king was "wicked" (12:17) and "evil" (12:20). The narrator puts the same words in the mouths of the people (12:19), as though they're confessing to

---

[13] This might also be a theological trauma response, given how culturally devastating Israel's defeat by the Babylonians was. I have perfect mental health though, so I can't evaluate this claim…just kidding. For better or worse, cultural trauma is a theologically productive force.

the charge. Obviously, they're not really, because then they'd simply get rid of the monarchy and live how Samuel wants them to, but they're actually quite happy with a king.

Samuel though, is not, and he's not about to let Saul rule in peace.

Samuel vs. Saul (1 Samuel 13–15)

The tension between Saul and Samuel ratchets up in 1 Samuel 13–15, as the newly appointed king returns his attention to the Philistines. Saul gathers his troops at Gilgal and waits seven days for Samuel to appear and offer a sacrifice to bless the battle to come. When Samuel doesn't show, Saul offers the sacrifice himself to rally his troops, only for Samuel to then appear and chastise Saul for his disobedience. Samuel tells Saul that his kingdom will not endure and that God has already sought out his replacement.

Saul's son Jonathan has military adventures of his own, defeating large numbers of Philistines by himself. But Jonathan accidentally violates an oath sworn by Saul, causing God to disapprove of Saul and refuse to speak to him.

Later, Samuel delivers a message from God to Saul, commanding him to enact genocide against the Amalekites. Saul does not fulfill this command thoroughly enough, causing Samuel to again condemn Saul and his rule. Chapter 15 ends with the narrator's comment that God regretted making Saul king.

Saul

Whoever wrote this section of 1 Samuel hates Saul. I don't really think there's any other way to think about it.

Chapter 13 begins by telling us Saul's age and the length of his reign, but the Hebrew text is missing words here, and we don't know what the numbers are supposed to be. Considering Saul was a young man in chapter 9 and he now has a son old enough to command his own military forces (13:2), it seems a considerable time has passed since Saul was first made king. Saul and his son successfully take out a Philistine garrison (13:2–4), but the feeling of victory is short-lived because the Philistines respond by raising an enormous army (13:5). Saul camps out at Gilgal, waiting for Samuel, as his troops begin to desert him out of fear of the Philistines (13:6–7).

It's standard practice in ancient Israel for an offering to be made to God on the eve of a momentous battle, but Samuel isn't there to do it. Saul waits seven days, and when Samuel doesn't show up, Saul offers the sacrifice himself in an attempt to salvage what remained of his army's morale (13:8–9). Just then, as if he were hiding in a bush nearby, Samuel pops out and scolds Saul for offering the sacrifice (13:13). Samuel goes on to tell Saul that his kingdom will not endure and that God is already seeking someone to replace him as king (13:14).

If this seems like a nonsensical and overly harsh punishment, you're not crazy. It doesn't make any sense. If you remember back to 1 Samuel 10:8, Samuel had instructed Saul to wait seven days at Gilgal for him so that he could arrive and offer a sacrifice. The problem is, this was *literally decades* ago in narrative time. Saul has no reason to think that, just because one time twenty years ago Samuel told him to wait at Gilgal for seven days, then *every time* he's thinking about offering a sacrifice at Gilgal he should wait seven days. But even worse, Saul *does* wait seven days! He doesn't disobey at all. Samuel said "wait." Saul waited. Samuel didn't show up when he said he would, so Saul took care of it. Saul's innocent, but Samuel and the author of this chapter disagree.

The author's real problem with Saul seems to be his concern for the practical elements of war, like his army's morale (13:11). Remember that the anti-monarchical voice thinks a king is unnecessary because God can just auto-win battles for Israel, so this voice finds Saul's vested interest in winning the battle in a conventional way to be distasteful. Apparently this voice would have preferred Saul to wait indefinitely for Samuel, totally apathetic to his army's desertion, since in the end God and not armies wins battles. Saul is punished for caring about his army, which is the entire point of a king in this context, and so, weirdly, Saul is punished for caring about being king.

Samuel tells Saul that God is already looking for a "man after his own heart" (13:14). This is our first reference to David, who will be chosen to be king after God looks at his heart (16:7) and who the New Testament remembers as a man after God's own heart (Acts 13:22). Why a person needs to have this quality of being after God's heart when God can just give a person a new heart with this quality (10:9) is not clear. How Saul demonstrates he doesn't have this quality by offering a sacrifice is unclear. How David has this quality is also unclear. Nothing is clear here except that the author hates Saul.

Jonathan

The next story introduces us more thoroughly to Jonathan, Saul's oldest son and the heir apparent. Jonathan is a heroic and pious man, as is evident by the fact that he goes to fight a Philistine garrison with only his armor bearer by his side, confident that God can give them victory regardless of their small number (14:6). We'll learn later that Jonathan is an honorable, deeply feeling, and loyal man as well. In comparison to the sons of Eli and Samuel, Jonathan is a knight in shining armor. It's reasonable to assume that his good qualities are at least in part the result of Saul's parenting. Saul, like his father before him, turned out to be one of the better parents in the story.

Jonathan's attack on the garrison is a success (14:14); the Philistines are thrown into a panic (14:15), and Saul is able to rally enough of his demoralized forces to put the Philistines to flight (14:20–23).

Two interesting details are worth noting in this section. The first is that God seems to help both Jonathan and Saul by initially panicking the Philistines in 14:15 and then by increasing the panic when Ahijah the priest brings the ephod, the special breastplate of the high priest, to the battle (14:18). Some translations will have the ark of the covenant here as the sacred object brought to the battle, but this is a later version of the story that doesn't match Ahijah's description in verse 3: "Ephod" is more likely original.

God even takes credit for the victory (14:23), as though God was acting through Saul and Jonathan. Again, we're struck by the juxtaposition of the Bible's multiple underlying voices. How can God take credit for the efficacy of the army when Samuel just punished Saul for caring too much about the efficacy of the army? There isn't an answer to the question. The text doesn't know either.

Another interesting detail is that some Israelites, referred to as Hebrews, had apparently gone over to the Philistines' side (14:21) but returned to the Israelites when the battle started to turn in Saul's favor. Why would some Hebrews, who are Israelites, fight alongside Israel's enemy? It could simply be cowardice and opportunism, but it could also be more intentional mercenary work. Tuck that possibility in the back of your mind. It'll come up again.

As much as Jonathan led the victory over the Philistines, he's about to lead his father into trouble. At some point, off camera, Saul had made an oath that no one in his army would eat until nightfall (14:24). Kind of a dumb move, but people make rash oaths when they're seeking revenge against ancestral enemies. Jonathan, hungry but having not heard Saul's oath, eats some honey (14:27). The rest of Saul's men soon follow suit, looting the Philistines, butchering their animals, and then eating these animals, blood and all (14:32). When it comes to Saul's attention that his men are eating animal blood (14:33), he attempts to prevent this taboo from being flouted by building an altar so the animals can be properly sacrificed and consumed without blood (14:35).[14]

But God isn't a fan of the men breaking Saul's rash oath, so when Saul tries to inquire of God as to whether he should pursue the Philistines further, God doesn't answer him (14:37).[15] Saul casts lots[16]

---

[14] Leviticus 17:10–14 explains the idea behind this taboo.

[15] Kinda petty tbh.

[16] Here we have the Urim and Thummim, which were the instruments of divination used by the high priest.

to determine who is responsible for God's lack of communication, and Jonathan's name comes up (14:41–42). Jonathan takes responsibility and honorably accepts death as a punishment (14:43), but Saul's men intervene and argue that Jonathan cannot be guilty since he was only able to achieve his victory because of God's help (14:45). Again the question is raised: is God opposed to Saul and Jonathan, or is God helping them?

Chapter 14 then ends with a summary of Saul's military career and the names of his family members. It's the kind of summary you'd expect to see at the end of a person's life; while Saul will survive all of 1 Samuel, the summary is setting us up to expect the end of Saul as we know him.

Samuel

The story continues in grim fashion with Samuel taking the reins of the army and ordering that Saul totally annihilate the Amalekites for centuries' old grievances that make little sense in the moment (15:1–2). Samuel's command is essentially unprovoked genocide, intended to eliminate all the Amalekite men, women, and children and even their animals (15:3).

The specific term used for the destruction of the Amalekites is *herem*, a Hebrew word sometimes translated as "the ban, "devotion to destruction," or "utter destruction." *Herem* is a kind of ritual warfare where everything killed or destroyed is understood as a sacrifice to God. The justification given for the practice of *herem* in Deuteronomy 20:17–18 is that the complete annihilation of a people and their property is necessary to prevent them from causing future idolatries.

Neither idolatry in general nor the Amalekites in particular have been an issue in the narrative thus far, making Samuel's command appear arbitrary. Like, what good is being achieved here? Given how the story is about to unfold, it feels a bit like a trap.

Saul summons the army (15:4) then dutifully murders every Amalekite man, woman, and child (15:7), leaving alive only the king and the best of the livestock (15:9) to be sacrificed to God (15:15). Again, we have a story where Saul appears compliant, but Samuel takes issue regardless. God tells Samuel that he regrets making Saul king because of his disobedience, and Samuel spends all night crying his eyes out (15:11) because Saul hasn't genocided hard enough.

Samuel confronts Saul, who insists multiple times he was obedient (15:13, 20–21), but as with the sacrifice at Gilgal, it doesn't matter. Samuel hates Saul, and Saul will never be innocent enough for him. In a moment of peak irony, Samuel asks Saul, "Does God delight in sacrifice as much as obedience?" (15:22). Considering that God set up the sacrificial system to begin with, that God was enticed to destroy the Philistines because of a sacrifice, that God likes sacrifices before every major battle in which a king engages, and that God commanded *herem*, which is itself a war of sacrifice, it seems like the answer to Samuel's question is "yes" rather than the implied "no." This is supposed to be a hard-hitting rhetorical question that reveals something Saul hadn't realized before, but it just shows the confusion of Samuel's charge against Saul. Sacrifice *is* obedience. Saul was always sacrificing *out of obedience*. Samuel had no good reason to condemn Saul, but he condemns Saul regardless.

Now, you might say, and rightfully so, "Wait wait wait, it's not Samuel condemning Saul, it's God. Samuel's just a prophet delivering God's message." But all prophecy is mediated through a human person— a person with their own theology and agenda. Samuel speaking to Saul on God's behalf is not identical to God speaking directly to Saul. One involves a human element, and the human element here is questionable.

Samuel's incoherent condemnation of Saul continues in the verses that follow. Having no luck arguing his innocence, Saul confesses to wrongdoing (15:24) and then begs for forgiveness so that he can worship God again on good terms (15:25). Samuel angrily rejects his plea (15:26) before telling Saul that God is giving the kingdom to someone better than him (15:28) and that Saul's pleas are irrelevant because God doesn't change his mind (15:29).

This, of course, is absurd. God has *literally* just had a change of mind. God chose Saul as king, *multiple times* mind you, then regretted that choice and chose someone else. If that's not changing your mind, then nothing is. Samuel's irrational reasoning throughout this confrontation—about sacrifice, about the possibility of forgiveness, about whether God changes God's mind—reveals the frailty of the human element in divine communication. Whatever God is trying to convey through Samuel, it's not really coming through in the midst of all this sloppy theology. What *is* coming through is Samuel's hatred of Saul.

The chapter ends with a bloody spectacle. Samuel cuts the Amalekite king into pieces at Gilgal as a human sacrifice (15:33), ironically fulfilling Saul's purpose in keeping him alive despite being punished for it. We're then told that Samuel returns to Ramah, the place of his birth, and Saul returns to his home (15:34–35). The men don't see each other again for the rest of Samuel's life, though through necromancy, they will speak a final time on the night before Saul's death.

Samuel is said to grieve over Saul, while God regrets having made Saul king. The line between Samuel's and God's emotions vanishes, and we're left to wonder if it ever existed. Like the end of an episode of Scooby-Doo, maybe Samuel was under the god-shaped mask all along.

CHAPTER THREE

David's Rise

David vs. Goliath (1 Samuel 16–17)

We're introduced to David in 1 Samuel 16 and 17—two different and frequently contradictory stories. In 1 Samuel 16, Samuel is directed by God to anoint one of Jesse's sons as king, and Samuel travels covertly to Bethlehem out of fear of reprisal from Saul. Once there, he anoints David as king in a private ceremony, prompting the spirit of God to come on David and an evil spirit to torment Saul. David is brought into Saul's service as a musician to soothe his paranoid outbursts.

In 1 Samuel 17, one of the most popular chapters in the entire Bible, we read about David's legendary confrontation with the Philistine giant Goliath. Goliath taunts Saul's army and demands single combat, but none of Saul's soldiers are brave enough to respond until David arrives. Though just a young man, David confronts Goliath with his sling and his faith in God, and he prevails over the giant. Afterwards, David is brought into Saul's service again.

David

Much like with the three independent stories of Saul becoming king, we're introduced to David in a pair of stories about how he joins Saul's household. Popular imagination often allows us to recall bits and pieces of these stories, but if we can hold both of them in our minds at once, we quickly see that they're full of contradictory details that almost guarantee they were composed at different times by different people and then edited together.

The narrative in 1 Samuel 16 picks up where 1 Samuel 15 left off, with God telling Samuel to stop grieving about Saul and go to the house of Jesse in Bethlehem to anoint one of his sons as king (16:1). We're told virtually nothing about Jesse. It's reasonable to infer that he's a politically connected elder, popular enough that David will frequently be referred to as the "son of Jesse," as though his dad is a big deal. Jesse's eight sons, his flocks that David tends, and his later job provisioning Saul's army imply that he's a man of means, but not much is made of this. The meaning of his name is somewhat mysterious as well. Jesse derives from the rather abstract Hebrew word *yesh*, which is used to indicate presence or possession. Frankly, it doesn't make a great name. It might mean something like "God exists," which is pious but kinda boring. We get very little sense of Jesse's character, either here or elsewhere, and that's unfortunate because I'd really like to know what kind of father he was. It might explain so much about David.

Samuel is initially concerned about traveling to anoint a new king out of fear that Saul will discover it and have him killed (16:2). This concern comes a bit out of left field. Samuel has loudly and publicly criticized Saul before, even in front of his army, without any apparent fear of retaliation. It's likely this comment foreshadows future changes in Saul's character.

Samuel arrives at Bethlehem under the pretense of offering a sacrifice (16:3), but the elders of the city greet him with fear (16:4), probably out of concern that he's come to condemn them for something they were unaware of. Over the next several verses (16:6–13), Jesse calls his sons one at a time to come before Samuel, who likely uses some instrument of divination like casting lots to discern which son is the one God has chosen to be king.

Samuel is initially certain that Jesse's oldest son, Eliab, is the one to be king, apparently because of his good looks and height like Saul before him. But God tells Samuel that God doesn't consider people's appearances, only their heart, harkening back to Samuel telling Saul that God was replacing him with a man after God's own heart. In a hilarious bit of irony, when all of Jesse's other sons have been considered and David is finally brought forward,[1] we're told that he's tan, pretty, and has beautiful eyes (16:12),[2] but we're not told anything about his heart that might qualify him over and above his brothers. Nevertheless, Samuel anoints David, whose name means "beloved," as king (16:13).

Using that familiar language from Judges and from Saul's third story of becoming king, the spirit of God comes powerfully upon David[3] and simultaneously departs from Saul only to be replaced by an evil spirit that makes him violent and paranoid (16:14). Saul's servants, operating with the ancient belief that music might drive away evil spirits, put out a call for musicians (16:15–17), and one of Saul's attendants recommends David (16:18).

This leads to a description of David that will be contradicted in the next chapter. David is said to be a "valorous warrior" and a "man of war" (16:18), who is quickly appointed to be Saul's armor-bearer (16:21) on account of Saul's great love for him. Kids can't be valorous warriors and men of war. David is imagined to be a grown man in 1 Samuel 16—the youngest of Jesse's sons, yes, but a grown man with military experience regardless. Skilled enough, in fact, to be Saul's armor-bearer, which was like a personal bodyguard. Keep that in mind.

Over the course of 1 Samuel 16, David goes from the son of a popular and potentially wealthy elder in a small city to an armor-bearer for the king. David is a member of Saul's inner circle, the king's household, upon whom Saul is utterly dependent on account of the evil spirit that

---

[1] Serious footnote for a change since I didn't know where else to put it. According to 1 Chronicles 2:15, David is Jesse's seventh son, where here in 1 Samuel 16:10 and following, he's the eighth. That's a contradiction. Is it an important one? No, probably not. That's why it's in a footnote.

[2] God might not look at people's outward appearance, but the narrator is looking, and he thinks David is hot.

[3] I'm certain this is unrelated to him being hot.

afflicts him. That's quite a promotion. David's life will be filled with such promotions, in which the suffering of others clears the way for his advancement.

It's a bit surprising to see David positioned in such a way by the close of 1 Samuel 16 because 1 Samuel 17 contains a different story about how David entered into Saul's household, and it's one that presumes David is both a child and unknown to Saul. It's also one of the most famous stories in the Bible. It's *also* largely a lie. Now I'm not saying it's a lie just to hold your attention and keep you turning pages,[4] but rather because, in two significant ways, we can see how the story has changed over time.

The story as it appears today is familiar even to many people who haven't read the Bible before. Israel goes to war with the Philistines (17:1–3), and a giant Philistine named Goliath challenges Israel's army to single combat (17:4–10). This is, understandably, terrifying (17:11). David is introduced for a second time, as though he hadn't been just a few minutes before, and he brings supplies from his home to his brothers on the Israelite front just in time to see Goliath come out and taunt the army (17:12–24).

Some brotherly quarreling follows (17:25–31) before David volunteers to fight Goliath. He then provides his questionable qualifications—killing animals while shepherding—as justification for being chosen (17:32–37). For some bizarre reason, Saul agrees. Unable to wear Saul's armor or wield his weapons, David goes out to fight Goliath with a staff and a sling (17:38–40). After some vicious boasts from Goliath and some pious boasts from David, David knocks Goliath prone with a stone from his sling and then cuts off his head with the soldier's own sword (17:41–51).[5] The Philistine army breaks and the Israelites carry the day (17:52–53).

---

[4] I'm not a monster.

[5] We're told that David takes Goliath's head to Jerusalem (17:54), which is about 20 miles northeast of where this battle is taking place and isn't controlled by the Israelites until 2 Samuel 5. As funny as it might be to imagine little David running a marathon into an enemy-occupied city to drop off

The story of David and Goliath then goes down in history as an archetypal example of faith triumphing over impossible odds.[6] But as I said before, there's some textual shenanigans happening here.

First, the story flatly contradicts 1 Samuel 16. In chapter 16, David is a valorous warrior and a man of war, but in chapter 17, David isn't strong enough or experienced enough to wear Saul's armor. Saul specifically says he can't fight because he's just a boy (17:33). A more egregious contradiction comes at the end of chapter 17, when Saul doesn't seem to know who David or his father are (17:55–58), despite having corresponded with Jesse to bring David into his service (16:22). This, combined with the redundant introduction to David, strongly suggests that chapters 16 and 17 were originally independent traditions about how David came into Saul's service. Either would be sufficient to explain this by itself, but both back-to-back cause contradictions.

Second, David probably didn't kill Goliath. Why would I say that?[7] Consider how many times Goliath is referred to by name in 1 Samuel 17. Only twice, in verses 4 and 23. On every other of nearly thirty occasions, he's simply referred to as "the Philistine." This is unusual. Like, so unusual there aren't any other examples of biblical narratives in which a prominent character is referred to by their ethnicity alone. What explains this unusual feature of the text? It might be because of another contradiction that's at stake in 1 Samuel 17. In 2 Samuel 21:15, in a list reviewing the accomplishments of some of David's elite soldiers, we're told that a man named Elhanan[8] killed Goliath. The description of Goliath in 2 Samuel 21 matches the description in 1 Samuel 17. There's no mistaking it. It's the same Goliath.

So who really killed Goliath? Well, what's more likely from a historical perspective? That David killed Goliath and then his great deed got attributed to one of his elite soldiers? Or that Elhanan killed Goliath

---

Goliath's head to a bunch of confused Jebusites, it's probably just the case that this reference is anachronistic.

[6] And of short kings triumphing over anything bigger than them.

[7] For dramatic effect, obviously.

[8] No relation to Elkanah, Hannah's baby daddy.

and then his great deed got attributed to his famous king? Obviously the latter.[9] It's probably the case that, originally, there was a story of David killing some unnamed Philistine, then, when Elhanan killed Goliath—a more impressive giant of a Philistine—some fan of David went back and added Goliath's name and description to 1 Samuel 17. A story about faith triumphing over tough odds then became a story of faith triumphing over impossible odds.

If this seems like a lot of speculation on my part, I understand where you're coming from. We tend to think of biblical texts as fixed things that people don't mess with. But I should point out that the version of 1 Samuel 17 we find in the Septuagint, the Greek translation of the Hebrew Bible, is missing many verses.[10] Most of these verses, like the introduction of David and Saul wondering who David is, are the verses that most obviously contradict the previous chapter. It looks like someone noticed the contradictions and decided to take these out. The Septuagint is what the authors of the Gospels read, so if you asked them how the story of David and Goliath went, they'd tell you a story without these contradictions. Weird, huh? People tinker with the Bible. You'll get used to it.

A final note to end on: first impressions matter. As I've said before, a character's first words often reveal something about who they are. We didn't get a chance to see what David's first words were in 1 Samuel 16, because David doesn't speak in 1 Samuel 16. He stays mute as he's anointed king. But we do get to see his first words in 1 Samuel 17. Drawing near to the frontline and hearing Goliath taunt the Israelite army, David asks, "What shall be done for the man who

---

[9] Another serious footnote. Interestingly, 1 Chronicles 20:5 tries to fix this contradiction by having Elhanan kill Lachmi, Goliath's supposed brother, but this is entirely made up. Some translations of 2 Samuel 21:15, like the popular NIV translation, will borrow the language from 1 Chronicles 20:5 and put it here to try to hide the contradiction. If you're reading an NIV Bible, don't. Treat yourself to a NRSV study bible. You deserve it.

[10] Specifically, verses 12–31, 41, 48b, 50, and 55–58.

kills this Philistine?" (17:26a). Or, put another way, "What can violence get me?"

David is introduced in 1 Samuel 17 as young, boastful, and most importantly, *ambitious*. Saul didn't want the throne. When the opportunity came, he demurred, then hid, then did what he had to do to save his people, but you never, ever, get the sense that he wanted to be king.

David wants it. David wants it *bad*, and he's ready and willing to ply his penchant for violence to get what he wants. And what's the reward for killing Goliath? Wealth and marriage to one of Saul's daughters (17:25b). Marriage to a princess would put a man within striking distance[11] of the throne. David only volunteers to kill Goliath after being told what the reward is. As pious as his stated motivations are (17:36–37), they are secondary to the reward. His older brother Eliab even calls him out on this (17:28), but David laughs off the rebuke (17:29).

With David we begin to see, perhaps more clearly than with Samuel, the conflation between the divine will and human will. Both Samuel and God didn't like Saul, but Samuel had a veneer of innocence because he didn't seem to have anything to gain by condemning Saul. Samuel might have been nostalgic for a time when he was in charge of Israel as a judge, but he didn't ever want the throne for himself.

David, on the other hand, wants the throne for himself, and his violent ambitions parallel God's desire to put him there. David will go on to kill a lot of people in the nineteen chapters it takes for him to be king. Is that what God wanted? It's a difficult question to ask and even harder to answer. Did God originally plan to put David on the throne by peaceful means but then David's inclination toward violence took over and he cut his way there? Or did God always plan to put David on the throne through David's own violent plotting? The text is open to either interpretation, and you may find yourself going back and forth as you turn the page and learn more about who David is.

---

[11] Literally.

Saul vs. David (1 Samuel 18–27)

David becomes a national war hero, beloved by both the public at large and by prominent people in Saul's household, like Saul's oldest son and heir, and his daughter. Saul grows increasingly paranoid and ruthless, promoting David to risker and risker positions in the military in the hope that foreign enemies will kill him off. But David has enormous success wherever he goes and sees his fame bolstered. When enemies don't get the job done, Saul attempts to kill David himself, but Saul's son and daughter find cunning ways to save David's life and allow him to escape unharmed.

David goes on the run, and after he deceives a community of priests into giving him provisions and arms, Saul arrives and has the priests slaughtered for colluding with David. David then attracts a band of fighting men to his side and grows in wealth as he extorts his fellow countrymen and cultivates ties with foreigners. On several occasions, Saul catches up with David, and David has the opportunity to kill the king, but he chooses to spare Saul's life for pious reasons. Eventually David isn't safe anywhere in Israel and he flees to Philistine lands, where he becomes a mercenary tasked with fighting his own people. But David lies, raiding Canaanite villages and then telling his Philistine overlords that he got the loot from Israelites.

Saul

The Saul we see for the rest of 1 Samuel is very different from the Saul we have known thus far. Saul was introduced to us as humble and a bit unfocussed. He worried about the feelings of his father, got distracted trying to recover his donkeys, and hid when he was made king; but then he finally rose to the challenge of defending Israel. Later, he fought whomever he needed to fight, all while Samuel bore down on him, and his son got him into trouble. He's never been a passive figure, but he was often reactive, trying to survive in the strange and dangerous circumstances in which he was thrust.

But when God sends an evil spirit to torment Saul following David's anointing (16:14)—a spirit that rears its ugly head again after the death of Goliath (18:10)—Saul is horrifically transformed into a man of singular focus. His entire life from here until his death becomes a prolonged and paranoid attempt to kill David. The tragedy of Saul's story is that every attempt he makes to take David's life only results in the alienation of his family and the growing power of David.

It starts simply. Despite his former love for David (16:21), when Saul hears women singing songs[12] celebrating David's victory over the Philistines (18:7), he becomes irrecoverably jealous of David and seeks to kill him (18:8–9). His first attempt is to throw a spear at David, but David escapes (18:10–11). Saul then attempts, twice, to have David killed in wars by promoting him in the army. The first time, David is made a commander of a thousand men and has enormous success, leading to the people of Israel and Judah loving him all the more (18:12–16).

The second time is more elaborate. Saul recalls that he had promised a daughter to whoever killed Goliath, but Saul's oldest, Merab, has already been married off to someone else (18:17–19). Seeing that his other daughter Michal loves David, Saul arranges a marriage between them (18:20–22). David demurs in light of the fact that marriage to a princess would require an enormous bride price that he is either unable or unwilling to pay (18:23). But Saul requests Philistine foreskins[13] as a bride price, again hoping that David will die in his attempt to acquire these (18:25–26). Saul chronically underestimates David's talent for violence, though, and David procures the foreskins and marries Michal (18:27–29). Despite Saul's attempts, chapter 18 ends with

---

[12] "Saul has killed his thousands and David his ten thousands." It's a bop, for sure. It's also false if 1 Samuel 17 is true, since David has only killed one person, Goliath. But hey, don't let the truth stop you from creating a hit.

[13] "Uncircumcised" was a common ethnic slur Israelite characters hurled at Philistines. Fortunately, the Philistines have thick skin.

David as a beloved commander of the army and now married into Saul's household.

Saul next attempts to bring his son Jonathan into his schemes, but because Jonathan is as enamored with David as everyone else, he warns David of his father's plans and scolds his father for his malicious intentions (19:1–5). This appears to have an effect on Saul, and he swears off trying to kill David (19:6), but God's evil spirit returns (19:9), and Saul immediately begins seeking David's life again.

Eventually, David is forced to flee from Saul's household and travels to Samuel at his home town of Ramah (19:18). Saul pursues him, but in a bit of dark comedy, both Saul's messengers and Saul himself collapse in a naked prophetic trance when they approach Samuel (19:19–24).

Undeterred, Saul continues to pursue David after he escapes again. David temporarily seeks shelter among the priests of a town called Nob. These priests are headed by Ahimelech, who is willing to offer David aid because he believes David is in Saul's service. If I told you that Ahimelech was the grandson of Eli, you could probably guess how the story is going to turn out.

When Saul hears of this, he summons all the priests of Nob to himself (22:11) and accuses them of assisting David despite David being against him (22:12–13). Ahimelech pleads his innocence, explaining that he thought David was on a mission for Saul (22:14–15), but Saul isn't convinced.

Insane with frustration, Saul has almost one hundred priests executed on the spot, and then he has all the inhabitants of Nob killed for good measure (22:18–19). A single priest named Abiathar escapes and goes to join up with David (22:20–23). These deaths and Abiathar's escape are further brutal echoes of the curse put on Eli's household back in 1 Samuel 2:31–33.

The curse turns out to be a rather strange bit of theology, considering all the coincidences that had to occur in order for it to be fulfilled. When God cursed Eli, did God know Saul would become king? That Saul would then fail for whatever reason and be replaced by David?

That Saul would then go crazy and try to kill David, even to the point of killing anyone who gave him aid? If God did, then why make Saul king to begin with? If God didn't, then how else could the curse have been fulfilled?

We should keep in mind that the authors of these texts are not writing about these events as they happen, but rather after the event. They have the benefit of hindsight. They know how events will turn out and who will end up on top, and so they know who to say has God's favor and who to say is cursed. They're doing theology like most of us do theology—in retrospect—when we reflect on our lives and try to find God's hand in what's happened. Having seen the whole story, it's easier for them to say, "Ah, God must have cursed this family, look at all the terrible things that happened to them," or, "Look at who prevailed, surely God must have been with them." And since the authors of 1 and 2 Samuel are less interested in portraying God as loving than they are in portraying God as sovereign over history, they're willing to make theological moves that might leave us with questions today.

Anyway, back to Saul trying to kill David. Saul isn't messing around anymore and is now openly at war with David, bringing his army with him to hunt David through the countryside (23:7–8). In 1 Samuel 23, Saul nearly catches David, but is forced to break off his pursuit when he gets word that the Philistines are attacking.

In 1 Samuel 24 and 26, David manages to sneak up on Saul, once in a cave and then at night. Both times, he is able to prove to Saul that he could have killed him if he wanted, but, taking the pious high ground, David tells Saul that it would be irreligious to take his life. In both instances, Saul has a moment of clarity, just as he did when Jonathan confronted him. Saul weeps and calls David his son (24:16, 26:21), expresses regret about what he has done (24:17, 26:21), and wishes David well in his future endeavors (24:20, 26:25). In 1 Samuel 24:21, Saul has David promise not to kill off his family when David becomes king, and in 1 Samuel 26:21, Saul himself promises not to try to hurt David again. Neither man keeps their promise.

These quiet moments of clarity, when Saul realizes what he has become, are quite sad when you think about it. Saul is the way he is because of the evil spirit God has set upon him. When Saul apologizes for what he has done, it feels like we are being given a glimpse of who Saul would be without that evil spirit's corrosive effects on his sanity. I think it's hard not to feel some measure of pity for Saul, but your mileage may vary.

After Saul's repeated attempts to kill David, what does he have to show for it? David is more popular than ever. A one-off anecdote relayed in 1 Samuel 22:2 says that a group of distressed and discontented people gather around David. Apparently there are plenty more people dissatisfied enough with Saul's rule to join up with David at great risk to themselves; and apparently there are enough fighting men among them for David to fend off a Philistine attack on a small town (23:1–5). Abiathar, the lone priest who escaped the slaughter of Nob, joins with David, giving him a degree of religious legitimacy. That's a big deal, because what else is a king but a successful military leader with religious legitimacy? Saul has done nothing but turn David into the very thing he feared he would become.

And what must hurt Saul the most is that even his children are on David's side.

Jonathan

When David kills Goliath and is brought into Saul's household, we're given a moving description of Jonathan's feelings toward David. Jonathan's soul is said to be bound to David's, and Jonathan comes to love him as himself (18:1–2). Jonathan then makes a covenant with David on account of this love, stripping himself of his robe and giving it to David along with his armor and weapons (18:3–4). We're not told about the content of this covenant, like what either party is agreeing to do for the other; nor are we told David's response. The narrator mentions the gesture as though the reader will understand what it means, and biblical scholars have argued ever since, unable to agree on what it means.

There are a few possibilities. It could be a political gesture. Jonathan, as the heir apparent, could be conceding the throne to David by giving him symbols of his kingship, such as the wealthy robe, arms and armor. Read in this way, Jonathan knows the second he sees David that David will be king, and Jonathan's love for David becomes a statement of political fealty. This would make Jonathan out to be a pious man who is able to recognize the person has God's favor.

It could be a fraternal gesture. Jonathan is welcoming David into his house as a brother in arms. Indeed, it is reasonable to assume that Jonathan fought side by side with David, given the prominent military positions they both held. We already know from Jonathan's introduction that he is a brave and skilled soldier. David and Jonathan could have that in common. Read in this way, Jonathan's love is one of intense commitment to fight alongside David in the battles to come.

It could be a romantic/erotic gesture. Jonathan is presenting himself to David, naked and vulnerable. This reading would account for the intensity of Jonathan's love, which is unprecedented in historical texts. Covenants can be political, but covenantal language is also the language of marriage. The only other places we see love described this strongly are in places like Ruth 1:16–17 (between Ruth and Naomi) and Song of Songs 2:16 (between two unnamed lovers). These verses relate the same complete commitment of self, described as a blurring of the line between the lover and the beloved. The Song of Songs verse is explicitly erotic, and some biblical scholars suspect the Ruth ones are as well, which would make the verses in 1 Samuel 18 more likely to be something similar.

Read in this way, we have a biblical expression of homoerotic desire and commitment. Against the possibility of this reading, we have the fact that such a relationship is (Ruth and Naomi aside) unattested in the Hebrew Bibles. Many would try to argue that the Hebrew Bible prohibits homoerotic relationships on the basis of passages like Leviticus 18:22 and 20:13, but 1 and 2 Samuel have no apparent knowledge of these laws—it's likely they hadn't been written yet.[14] Still, given the cultural mores of the time, we should be careful in presuming too much. At the same time, it is an unprecedented description, and so an unprecedented explanation is warranted.

In favor of this reading, I'd like you to consider two additional points of evidence.[15] The first is that Jonathan acts like David's wife. In what sense, you ask?[16] In 1 Samuel 19:8–17 and in the whole of chapter 20, we have two stories in which a character who loves David uses cunning to save David's life from Saul. The first story involves David's actual wife, Michal, who helps David flee out a window when Saul's assassins draw near. Michal then makes a little doll with an idol and some goat hair and puts it in bed so it looks like David is lying sick there.

The second story involves Jonathan concocting a plot to use arrows to signal to David whether it's safe for him to attend a new moon feast (and it's at this feast where Jonathan eventually learns Saul is planning to ambush David). This story also involves a breathless private conversation between Jonathan and David, where David recognizes that Saul is trying to use Jonathan's love for David against him (20:3) and where David swears on his love for Jonathan to take care of his household should Jonathan die (20:14–17).

These two stories parallel each other thematically, and it's in that parallel that the comparison between Michal, an actual wife, and Jonathan, who is playing the part of a wife, is made.

The second piece of evidence in favor of a romantic/erotic reading can be found in Saul's eventual condemnation of Jonathan. When Saul discovers that Michal saved David's life, he berates her (19:17), but when he discovers Jonathan saved David's life, he screams insults at

---

[14] The so-called Holiness Code (Leviticus 17–26) is often dated by biblical scholars to the Babylonian Exile (587–539 BCE) or even later.

[15] There's actually a third piece of evidence, but I don't want to spoil it for you yet. When we get there, I'll remind you. Don't worry.

[16] Good question.

him and then tries to kill him (20:30–33). The insult Saul chooses is telling: "You son of a perverse rebel! Do I not know that you have chosen the son of Jesse to your own shame and to the shame of your mother's nakedness?" (1 Samuel 20:30)

This can be read in two ways. First, Jonathan's mother, Ahinoam, is a rebellious woman, and so her son is as well. Jonathan's betrayal of Saul for David amounts to rebellion and shames his mother's nakedness in the sense that he was born to be king but has traded it away. Second, Ahinoam is a perverse woman, and so her son is as well. Jonathan's romantic love for David amounts to perversity and shames his mother's nakedness in the sense that he has done sexually illicit things that tarnish the family's honor. It's this second possibility that supports the romantic/erotic reading of Jonathan's love.

I think it's beyond our ability to prove that Jonathan and David had a romantic/erotic relationship, but I also don't think the possibility can be ruled out. There truly is no other relationship in biblical narrative described in this way. You can go check, and you'll realize how little love is mentioned in other relationships. Did Abraham love Sarah? I hope so, but the text doesn't say. Did Moses love Zipporah? Who knows? How does the Bible describe Jacob's feelings toward Rachel, the feelings powerful enough to make him work fourteen years for her? Genesis 29:20 says the years felt short to him because of his love.

That's it. It went by quick. 'Cause he loved her.

Cool.

That's nothing in comparison to what we have here, with love being repeatedly declared, souls merging, covenants and oaths being made, naked bodies, and secret rendezvous.

The text remains forever open to being read in a way that acknowledges something romantic/erotic between Jonathan and David. And for LGBTQ+ people, their allies, and the religious communities they are a part of, any possibility of biblical representation can be a life-giving thing and, I think, worth mentioning.

I can't think of a good segue, but I really should circle back to the part where Saul throws a spear at Jonathan (20:33). In Jonathan,

Saul managed to raise a heroic, pious man with a capacity for deep feeling and an enduring sense of loyalty to the ones he cares about. As a result, I'm willing to say Saul was a decent father. But just as the evil spirit turned him into a paranoid and violent man, it also stole away whatever healthy fatherhood he had in him, and Jonathan bears the brunt of that.

As I mentioned earlier, Saul attempts to get Jonathan in on killing David (19:1–4), and Jonathan is able to talk him out of it. But here, Saul insults Jonathan and tries to kill him. In response, Jonathan storms off (20:34).

Jonathan and David do get to say goodbye, though. When Jonathan comes to warn David about his father's attempt to ambush him, David bows to him, they kiss, and then they weep together, knowing they will be parted (20:41). Jonathan only leaves after they reaffirm their everlasting commitments to one another, as you might expect a couple to do. After this story, we hear nothing about Jonathan again until the day of his death. He appears in no scenes, either with his father or with David, implying a serious rupture with the former.

I should also point out that Saul is a terrible father to Michal as well. While Saul is aware of Michal's love for David, he doesn't arrange a marriage between them out of deference to his daughter's feelings but rather as a trap to have David killed off while seeking his gruesome bride price.

Saul instrumentalizes both Jonathan and Michal, attempting to use them as tools to further his goals and then discarding them when they no longer serve their purposes. This is bad, obviously, and while we're unlikely to fling spears at our kids,[17] we must still guard against more conventional kinds of manipulation which are no more justifiable.

---

[17] For lack of a spear, if nothing else.

David

While Saul is trying to kill David and while Jonathan is trying to stop that from happening, David himself is on quite a journey. Between the slaying of Goliath in 1 Samuel 17 and the end of the book, David goes from being no one of importance to being one of the most powerful people in the country.

God's presence in these stories is quite subtle. While God is still sending the evil spirit that drives Saul to try to kill David (19:9), God is also sending spirits that prevent Saul from being able to do just that (19:23). Otherwise, God's interactions with David during this period primarily take the form of responding to his attempts at divination, which again, probably involves something like casting lots for "yes or no" answers. David uses divination to ask God whether he should fight the Philistines (23:2–4) and the Amalekites (30:8); and the prophet Gad, presumably speaking on God's behalf, warns David when he must flee from Saul (22:5). But, as they say, that's largely that. There's little God and a lot of David in these stories, and so we get to see what kind of man he is when left to his own devices.

When David first leaves Jonathan in the aforementioned intimate scene, he travels to Nob, where the also aforementioned slaughter of priests by Saul will take place. But before said slaughter occurs, David has an interesting interaction with Ahimelek, the priest in charge of the sanctuary there, revealing himself to be a self-interested liar who isn't afraid of endangering innocent bystanders.

David lies to the priest, telling him that he is on a secret mission from Saul, when he is in fact running for his life from Saul (21:2). And then he uses the pretext of this secret mission to get supplies from the sanctuary (21:3).[18]

Ahimelek hesitates in providing food to David because it's been consecrated, and only someone who is ritually pure can touch it (21:4).

---

[18] He also takes Goliath's sword (21:9). So from here on out, any time you picture David fighting, you should picture him hauling around a giant-ass sword.

The main issue at stake is whether David has had sex recently, as sex confers a temporary ritual impurity to its participants.[19] David assures the priest that he is pure (21:5), and while it's impossible to know for sure, this is probably also a lie. David just left Michal two chapters ago, and we know from later chapters that he's traveling with his other wife Ahinoam (27:3).

Regardless of whether this is one lie or two, it's difficult to imagine that David didn't know the danger he was putting the priest in. Saul is actively looking to kill David. What was Ahimelek going to say to Saul when the king found out he aided and abetted a fugitive? Is Saul the kind of man, at this point in his life, to be chill about such a thing? No. While Saul's slaughter of literally everyone in Nob is a big deal, even for him, David must have known some harm would fall on Ahimelek's household for helping him.

We also learn that David is a bit of a freedom fighter, or at least, people rally around him thinking he is. When David's family hears he's on the run, they join him (22:1), which speaks well of those relationships. We also hear that many people who are in debt or facing other kinds of hardships gather to David (22:2), giving David a bit of a Robin Hood vibe. It is likely a poor reflection on Saul's rule that such a large number of people are willing to throw their lot in with an outlaw. The gathering of people includes four hundred men.

These men, and their ability to fight, play an essential role in several stories that follow. It's because of these men that David is able to save the city of Keilah from the Philistines in chapter 23 and to outmaneuver Saul in chapters 24 and 26. And it's because of these men that

---

[19] My editor would like me to point out that ritual purity and impurity don't have any moral connotations in these texts. Being pure doesn't mean you're good and being impure isn't bad. Ritual impurity could result from all sorts of conventional activities and sometimes it was even obligatory. Contemporary rhetoric about sex being impure and therefore sinful have no basis in these texts. It's an important point to make, since so many people have been hurt by rhetoric like this, and I'm grateful for her suggestion.

David is able to run a protection racket in the wilderness in chapter 25, where we also learn that David has a predatory eye for women.

Let's set the scene. David is in the wilderness near Carmel with his modest army of now six hundred (25:2),[20] and there's a rich man living in the area named Nabal.[21] David sends some young men to tell Nabal that the entire time David has been around, Nabal has been safe, so Nabal should compensate David with anything he asks (25:5–8). Basically, David could have killed him, but has graciously chosen not to, so pay up.

Apparently oblivious to the meaning of his unfortunate name, Nabal makes a foolish choice to tell David to go to hell (25:10–11).[22] David then tells his men to get their swords and he rides down to shishkabab Nabal (25:12–13).[23]

This is where we're introduced to Abigail, Nabal's wife, who hears about the exchange of messages. Abigail packages up a huge amount of food (25:18) and heads off in secret to intercept David (25:19). She spends nine laborious verses saying and doing everything a woman can to de-escalate a violent and prideful man (25:23–31), and in so doing, she saves her household. The next morning, when Abigail tells Nabal what happened, he has something like a stroke and then dies ten days later (25:26–28). David immediately sends for Abigail to make her his wife (25:39–42).

Abigail has absolutely no say in this situation, though some translations try to make it seem like she does. For example, the NIV renders this line, "Then David sent word to Abigail, asking her to become his wife."[24] The original Hebrew has no such connotation, saying literally

---

[20] This isn't the famous Mount Carmel where Elijah has his god-duel with the prophets of Baal in 1 Kings 18. That's in northwestern Israel. This is in southeastern Judah. Don't worry, I always get them mixed up, too.

[21] His name means "fool." That's a good indication he's going to die.

[22] I'm paraphrasing.

[23] This would be a good opportunity to picture that giant-ass sword.

[24] Lol why are you reading the NIV? Go to Amazon right now and buy the New Oxford Annotated Bible with the NRSV translation. You can thank me later.

"And David spoke with Abigail to take her as a wife for him." That's it. There's no *asking*. David does not say "please." David speaks and she is taken.

Abigail's response is one of utter submission, and it's kinda scary if looked at in a particular light. She says "Here is your maid, to serve and to wash the feet of the servants of my lord." The word "maid" here, which you'll see in many translations, is more properly thought of as an enslaved woman. Hagar is called a "maid" in this sense when she is given to Abraham to bear a child for Sarah (e.g., Genesis 21:10, 12–13). Enslaved women were at the disposal of their masters for both sexual and physical violence (e.g., Exodus 21:7, 20). The phrase "to wash the feet of" can be a euphemism for sex, too (e.g., 2 Samuel 11:18). Abigail's use of this language signifies that she understands what David is taking her for, and while we can't pretend to mindread characters in biblical narratives, it's difficult to imagine that Abigail is anything other than apprehensive about this proposition. She is working to save her life, not to run off with a man she loves.

If this were the only time that David used his position of domination to pluck a woman away from her husband, we might explain it as a one-off error in judgment. But as we will continue to see, it's actually David's preference to take women in this way. He develops quite a habit of it.

Back to Nabal for a second. Nabal's miraculously timed death is, as the kids say, suspicious af. He dies exactly when he needs to die so that David can step in and take control of his wealthy lands and so that David can steal away Abigail to add to the list of wives he's taken from other men.[25] If someone told you this story in some other context

---

[25] Keeping track is quite a task. Michal, given to David by Saul, is then given to another man when David flees, and then she's taken back by David after Saul's death. That's one. We're told David is already married to a woman named Ahinoam. That happens to be the name of one of Saul's wives. Is it the same woman? We can't know for sure, but it seems to be David's style, so I think it is. That's two. Now we have Abigail. That's three. We'll hit at least four before the story is done, maybe more.

besides the Bible, you'd probably suspect that Abigail killed Nabal in the middle of the night to save her household from being annihilated by David's personal army. Is that what happens here? Well, we're told that God strikes down Nabal (25:28). But this wouldn't be the first time the text attributes deaths to God that are actually caused by people (e.g., 1 Samuel 14:23).

A final thing we learn about David during these latter sections of 1 Samuel is that he is ready and willing to make peace with traditional enemies of the Israelites. While David is gallivanting around the countryside, he leaves his father and mother with the king of Moab (22:3–4), demonstrating a close bond between them despite how acrimonious conflicts with the Moabites can be.[26] David also twice joins up with the Philistines, once for a short stay in 21:10–15 where he feigns madness and once for an extended period in chapter 27 when he becomes a mercenary.

It's easy to gloss over David's mercenary days, probably because they're so at odds with the picture of David in popular memory. David is remembered as the slayer of the Philistine giant Goliath, not as a traitor who abandons his people to go fight for the Philistines. Yet the story spends more time describing the latter than it does the former. His time as a mercenary is also essential for understanding how he becomes king of Judah, which is something we'll explore in greater detail in the next section.

David resettles near the Philistine city-state of Gath with his family for more than a year (27:3, 7), and Achish, king of Gath, gives David a city (27:6), adding to his growing wealth. Once David moves to Gath, Saul gives up pursuit of him (27:4) since he is still at war with the Philistines. From Saul's perspective, David has gone over to the enemy. It's difficult to disagree. But David is exactly where he wants to be. If the king of Israel is at war with the Philistines and David is

---

[26] This might be part of the reason why a tradition develops that David has Moabite ancestry, a tradition we see in the biblical text at the end of the book of Ruth, where it is revealed that she, a Moabite, is David's great grandmother.

now part of the Philistine army, then David is only one step away from gaining the throne for himself.

Samuel vs. Saul Again (1 Samuel 28–2 Samuel 1)

Before a definitive battle with the Philistines, Saul attempts to inquire of God but receives no answer. So he seeks out a necromancer to bring up the soul of Samuel from the underworld to inquire of him instead, whereupon Samuel informs Saul of his fate. The next day, Saul and his son Jonathan die in battle against the Philistines. David, having used the wealth he has gained during his time as a mercenary to bribe the elders of Judah, is then named king over Judah after Saul's death.

Saul

You may be surprised to see Samuel's name in the title of this section. After all, we were told he died in chapter 25, and we're told again in 28:3 just in case we'd forgotten. Samuel is in fact dead.

Well then, you might ask,[27] how can there be any conflict between Samuel and Saul in chapter 28 if Samuel is dead?

Hold on to your Bibles, because I've got an answer for you and it's pretty crazy.

The Philistines advance on northern Israel, and Saul's army sets up camp nearby just southwest of the Sea of Galilee along the Jezreel Valley (28:4). Saul does exactly what he's supposed to do prior to entering a significant battle like this: he inquires of God to get God's permission/blessing to fight. Except God does not answer Saul through any licit means of divination (28:6).

Saul is then forced to seek out illicit means of getting God's permission/blessing to fight. We were told back in 28:3 that Saul had previously expelled all of the mediums from Israel, a comment

---

[27] Good, keep those questions up.

that probably didn't seem to mean very much at the time. But now it becomes central to the tension of the story, as Saul asks his servants to find such a medium (28:7). His servants find a woman at nearby Endor, and Saul visits her in disguise (28:8).

The medium is able to call up Samuel's soul from the underworld, and Saul asks Samuel what he should do (28:15). Samuel tells Saul that, because he failed to eradicate the Amalekites back in chapter 15, he's going to lose to the Philistines. Not only that, he and his sons are going to die, and the Israelite army will be destroyed (28:16–19).

We should probably pause for a moment and reflect on what just happened here. A woman, often called the witch of Endor, is able to summon Samuel's soul from the underworld. This single line is bursting with potential theological significance.

The woman can, apparently, do this at will and under her own power. The text does not say God did this for her. It's not a miracle, like when God threw the Philistines into disarray for Samuel back in chapter 7. Nor does the text say the woman could only do this because of some demonic contract with evil forces. None of that is happening here. Instead, as far as this story is concerned, this is an act of human-initiated *magic*. I'll bet you didn't expect Harry Potter to be on your Bible bingo card.

This passage also has significance for the author's beliefs about death. In 28:15, Samuel says he has been "disturbed by being brought up." We can infer several things from this. One, the author of this passage does not think the dead are either in a state of hellish torment or heavenly bliss, but rather something like sleep that a person can be disturbed and woken up from. Two, since being "brought up" from below is the only option either Saul or the medium discusses, the author of this passage thinks everyone goes to the same, generic underworld when they die. This is the conventional view of death throughout most of the Hebrew Bible, but it might be unfamiliar to readers who have later theologies of conscious punishment and reward in the afterlife.

Now, does the fact that there is magic and a sleepy underworld in this story mean there is magic and a sleepy underworld in real life?

That's more of a theological question (about what's actually true) than a biblical question (about what biblical authors and audiences convey and understand), and it's far beyond the scope of this little book to answer it. But I should point out that just because the Bible has a story about something, it doesn't mean it needs to play a role in our theology today. (And just because something *isn't* in the Bible, it doesn't mean it can't play a role in your theology.) You have the freedom as a reader of the text to decide if magic and this kind of afterlife are real or not.

Following his encounter with the medium, there is little left of Saul's life. His armies go to war with the Philistines (31:1). He watches as three of his sons, Jonathan included, are killed in battle (31:2). Saul himself is wounded by an arrow (31:3), and rather than fall into enemy hands to be shamefully tortured, he asks his shield bearer to kill him (31:4). The shield bearer can't bring himself to do it, however, and so Saul takes his own life. Thus ends the reign of Saul.

David

Chapters 29 and 30 of 1 Samuel go out of their way to establish that David, although he is an enormously successful warrior and loyal mercenary of the Philistines, was not there at the battle where Saul died. The text doth protesteth too much. No one in the world has as much to gain from the death of Saul as David, and there's no more logical place for David to be than at the very battle where Saul dies. Yet, so that we don't suspect David, the text provides a convenient alibi.

In response to the question, "Well, where was David during the battle?" chapter 29 explains that, despite David's year of service, the Philistine commanders (besides Achish) don't trust him. They won't allow him to take part in the battle with Saul, and so David returns to the city of Ziklag.

In case someone asks the follow up question, "Well, what was David doing at Ziklag during the battle?" chapter 30 answers by explaining that Ziklag had been attacked and looted by the Amalekites in David's absence. David is able to pursue the attackers, kill them, and recover all of his lost goods (31:17). Good for him.

Chapter 30 concludes with a curious note about how David spent some of that loot. The last six verses of the chapter are a list of town elders in Judah with whom David shares his wealth. What inspires this sudden act of generosity? David has never previously expressed an interest in rewarding random people with his wealth. If anything, he extorts people like Nabal for more. But David is a strategic man. He's investing in his future. And we'll see his investment pay off in just a short time.

But before any of that, we have one more glimpse of the David we saw back in 1 Samuel 20—the David who bows down before Jonathan and who kisses and weeps with Jonathan. In 2 Samuel 1, David hears of Saul's death from an Amalekite soldier who served in Saul's army (1:2). The soldier relates a very different death from the one we just heard about in 1 Samuel 31:4. In that story, Saul takes his own life with a sword after his shield bearer refuses. In this story, the soldier says he found Saul still alive after the battle (1:6–7). Saul asked him to take his life (1:9), and the soldier obeyed. As I said before, no one benefits more from the death of Saul than David, and yet David is incensed to hear of Saul's death. David has the soldier killed on the spot (1:15).

The rest of the chapter, verses 17–27, record the Lament of the Bow. David sings a song memorializing the death of Saul and Jonathan, and he orders all of Judah to learn the song so that it can be recited in perpetuity.

The lament begins with evocative nature imagery, as though the world itself has joined David in his grief (1:20–21). The middle section heaps praises on Saul and Jonathan as mighty, magnanimous, and loved (1:22–24), and the song concludes with special attention given to David's affection for Jonathan (1:25–27). The cumulative effect of the song is quite moving, and David's sense of loss is palpable. The final section concerning Jonathan has the provocative line that David's love for Jonathan was greater than the love of a woman (1:26), a final indicator of how unprecedented their relationship was.

And yet it's difficult not to see propaganda and embellishment in the song. Calling Saul "beloved" (1:23) seems hollow coming from the mouth of someone whom Saul tried to kill on several occasions, not to mention someone who has been maneuvering to supplant Saul as king. Verse 24 describes Saul as clothing the women of Israel in finery, as though his rule was particularly prosperous. But David attracted hundreds to his side because they were economically distressed under Saul's rule (1 Samuel 22:2). Any kindness David extends to Saul and Jonathan is tempered by the fact that David abandoned his people, became a Philistine mercenary, and was disappointed when he couldn't go to battle against Saul and Jonathan (1 Samuel 29:8).

The song on David's lips perfectly captures the kind of man he is in 1 and 2 Samuel: a deeply feeling man, capable of intense affection and a kind of abstract loyalty, but who nevertheless selfishly and brutally annihilates anything between him and his obsessive ambition.

David vs. Abner (2 Samuel 2–5)

With the death of Saul and his oldest son Jonathan, a power vacuum opens in Israel. With some politicking, assassinations, and a heaping pile of plausible deniability, David is able to eliminate what remains of Saul's household and clear his path to a monarchy centered on the city of Jerusalem.

David

There's a fair amount of subtle political maneuvering in 2 Samuel 2–5, which is very easy to gloss over when we don't understand the characters, their relations, and what's expected in the ancient cultural context. It might be helpful to lay out a road map before we dive in.

By the beginning of 2 Samuel 2, David is king over Judah, the southern portion of the greater Israelite territories, but the northern territories have remained loyal to the surviving members of Saul's household. If David wants to be king over the entirety of Israel's tribes and territories (and of course he does), then he needs to eliminate this remnant of Saul's household without looking like a megalomaniacal villain. Simply butchering Saul's last relatives would negatively dispose northern Israel to him, so David has to find some clever way to accomplish his goals while avoiding any public responsibility for them.

The two main targets David needs to eliminate are Abner, Saul's general, and Ishbaal,[28] Saul's oldest remaining son. Fortunately for David, Abner is ambitious and Ishbaal is weak, so the narrative between chapters 2 and 5 will involve David leveraging these flaws to bring about their deaths.

One more person needs to be introduced at this point. Apart from David, he is the single most important character for the remainder of 2 Samuel: David's nephew, Joab. Joab was first mentioned off-handedly in 1 Samuel 26:6 as the brother of Abishai, one of the men who helped David sneak up on Saul. Joab fought in David's mercenary band and is an incredibly skilled fighter. He wins every battle he's in, frequently with dramatic flourishes the author can't help but describe. Joab will become David's general, but he's much more than that. He's David's confidante and co-conspirator, David's enforcer and consigliere, and the closest thing to a friend David has.

In 2 Samuel 2:8–32, there is an elaborate but gapped narrative in which Joab and some of David's men spar against Abner and some of his men (2:12–15). What seems to start as a jocular exercise quickly becomes violent, and David's men kill many of Abner's (2:16–17). Then, in a running skirmish, Abner's men retreat and regroup with a larger force (2:18–25). Eventually, Abner and Joab decide to call it all off (2:26–28).

---

[28] Depending on your translation, you may see Ishbaal's name as Ishbosheth. Ishbaal means "man of Baal," and Baal is a Canaanite deity. Later scribes removed the name "Baal" because they opposed Baal worship/veneration, and replaced it with *bosheth* (Hebrew for "shame") to make Ishbosheth, meaning "man of shame."

We're not given any information about the motivation of these characters, either for arranging the sparring to begin with or for the resulting fighting. But one of the long-term consequences of this fighting is the death of Asahel, one of Joab's brothers, who's killed by Abner in the skirmish (2:23). This death turns out to be a key step toward David's goals.

In chapter 3, we're told that Saul's household is in decline, and it's in that context that Abner makes a play for power over northern Israel. He sleeps[29] with Rizpah, a woman who had been one of Saul's concubines (3:7). Sleeping with the wives and/or concubines of a man, living or dead, sends a message that you intend to replace that man. When Abner sleeps with Rizpah, he's telling everyone in northern Israel that he's replacing Saul as king. Abner was the one who had made Ishbaal king over northern Israel to begin with back in 2:9. For Ishbaal to lose Abner's support is devastating, and although Ishbaal tries to call Abner out for this, he's ultimately too afraid of the man to do anything about it (3:11). As well he should be. Abner is a general and a trained killer. Ishbaal is just some pampered princeling.

Abner, seeing the weakness of Ishbaal as a puppet king, conspires with David to secure a more viable future for himself (3:12). Abner offers David the support of northern Israel, and while the text never explicitly states what Abner wants in return, it seems reasonable to infer that he wants a safe and comfortable position in David's household. David agrees if he can have Michal, Saul's daughter, who had been his wife before but had been given to another man when David fled the country and joined the Philistines (3:13–16). This too is a political maneuver, as David's marriage to Michal was the original sign of his membership in Saul's household and gives him a degree of legitimacy as Saul's successor.

Abner agrees. Michal is transferred[30] to David, and Abner sends messages to the elders of Israel, hyping up David as king (3:17). Abner

---

[29] This is a euphemism. Rizpah has absolutely no say in the matter.
[30] Another euphemism, for much the same reason.

then comes to David at Hebron to celebrate their arrangement (3:20), but after Abner is dismissed, Joab arranges a secret meeting with him where he stabs him to death (3:27). The rest of the chapter is David loudly and publicly decrying Joab's actions, characterizing it as vengeance for the death of Asahel and condemning Joab as violent and uncontrollable. David washes his hands off the killing, saying he was "powerless" to do anything about it (3:39). The facts of the matter are that Joab is David's creature and that Asahel's death is a convenient excuse to deflect from the political motivation behind Abner's assassination. The chapter ends with David saying Joab and his brothers are too violent for him; but a few chapters later, Joab will be promoted to general. So we see how he really feels in time.

With Abner dead and the elders of Israel on David's side, the only obstacle left is Ishbaal. When Ishbaal hears that Abner is dead, he knows he's not long for the world (4:1). Two of his own captains, probably thinking they could get some deal with David,[31] kill Ishbaal in his sleep and bring his head to David (4:4–8). With the deed already done, David has no pragmatic reason to reward the captains, and so he feigns offense and has them executed on the spot (4:9–12).

The dawn of 2 Samuel 5 sees no more obstacles between David and the throne of Israel. His enemies are dead, and he has plausible deniability at every step. This is some *Game of Thrones* stuff and a testament to the combined cunning and ruthlessness of David and Joab. One might wonder, theologically, if this is what God had in mind back when Samuel anointed David king. David seems to undertake these actions at his own initiative. It's his ambition leading the way. If this is also God's will, then are God's will and David's ambition identical? The text doesn't attempt to answer this nuanced question, as much as we might want it answered.

The next chapter is largely a victory lap. David is made king over a united northern Israel and southern Judah (5:1–5); Jerusalem is conquered and, with contributions from the king of Tyre in Phoenicia,

---

[31] Apparently they weren't smart enough to learn from Abner's mistake.

made David's new capital (5:6–16); and the lingering threat of the Philistines is put down (5:17–25). David even manages to capture Philistine idols after the battle (5:21), finally getting revenge for the stolen ark and showing that Israelites were happy to engage in god-napping when they could. With David established, his anointing by Samuel way back in 1 Samuel 16 has come to full fruition.

Israel finally has a king that is a "man after God's own heart."

David vs. God (2 Samuel 6–9)

David brings the ark of the covenant to Jerusalem, a dangerous pro-cess that costs a life and results in a breakdown of the relationship between David and his recently returned wife Michal. The prophet Nathan arrives to inform David that he won't be the one to build God a temple, but instead God will establish a unique and everlasting cov-enant with him and his descendants. Chapters 8 and 9 focus on the administration of David's kingdom, battles won and political appoint-ments made, before concluding with a brief narrative of David taking in Saul's remaining son.

Michal

Having conquered Jerusalem and made it the political capital of his new united monarchy, all that's left for David to do is to also make it the religious capital as well. David attempts to accomplish this by moving the ark of the covenant to Jerusalem. David assembles a small army's worth of men[32] and travels to Baale-judah (6:1–2), which is another name for Kiriath-jearim where the ark was last seen in 1 Samuel 7. The ark is loaded into a cart, just like when it was transported by the

---

[32] The number given here is 30,000, but sometimes the Hebrew word for thousand can mean a military unit instead, so, 30 units.

Philistines, and David and his men give the ark a full musical procession as it makes its way to Jerusalem (6:3–5).

Just like when it was transported by the Philistines, the ark is a dangerous representation of God's presence, and when a man named Uzzah steadies the ark to stop it from falling, he's instantly killed by God (6:6–7). David is both frightened and angered by this turn of events, and he decides to abandon the ark at the house of a Philistine man, likely someone David knew from his mercenary days (6:8–10). But when the man's household is blessed by the presence of the ark, David loads up the ark again and brings it all the way to Jerusalem (6:11–15).

One of the most unique parts of this story is how the narrative shifts back and forth between David's perspective and Michal's. We don't often get female-centric points of view, but we do here, and it's especially significant because it's a point of view that's critical of David. As David brings the ark into Jerusalem, we're told that Michal spots him from a window. When she sees him dancing, she gets the "ick," as the kids say, and "despises David in her heart" (6:16). Michal had previously expressed her love for him in 1 Samuel 18:20, but now she has a variety of reasons to no longer like him. David left her after she saved his life, joined the enemy that killed her father, took a half dozen more wives, and then broke up her new marriage to force her back to his side.

But here, it's David's dancing that causes her adverse reaction. When David gets close to his home, Michal comes out and reprimands him. Her complaint is complex. She says David is honoring himself and that he has shamelessly uncovered himself before his servants' maids. The idea that David is honoring himself probably has to do with the elaborate series of public sacrifices he offers when the ark arrives in the city, coupled with the large amounts of expensive foods he distributes to the whole population (6:17–19). Both of these are lavish celebrations that increase his prestige in the eyes of common people and help cement his status as king after a violent rise to power.

The idea that David is shamelessly uncovering himself probably has to do with his garment—a linen ephod (6:14), which is like an apron and so wouldn't stay in place while David was leaping, dancing, and walking up to platforms and altars to offer sacrifices. David would be nearly as naked as Michaelangelo's statue of him. Public nudity in general would be shameful, all the more so in front of the young women Michal points out. This explains why she compares David to a vulgar person.

I'd like to think that Michal is also calling attention to David's reputation with women. The maids she references may not simply be the young women servants who happen to be present; instead, she could be using the term "maids" in the more euphemistic sense of any woman in the crowd who David might have his eyes on. Recall that Abigail referred to herself as a maid to convince David of her submissiveness and save herself. If Michal is referring to maids in this sense, then her criticism is of David's very visible promiscuity. Michal might not like it when David shows off for women whom he might turn into his eighth or ninth wives.

David responds by saying he wasn't dancing before any maids but before God—the same God who replaced Michal's father with him as king (6:21). David then says he won't stop and that he'll be honored by the same maids to whom Michal is referring (6:22). David's response makes the euphemistic interpretation of Michal's reprimand more likely. If David's actions were purely pious, then it would make sense for him to respond to Michal by saying God will continue to honor him. Instead, David makes sure to conclude by saying that women love him. Indeed, we're only a few chapters away from David snatching away another wife.

But when read theologically, we can squeeze even more meaning out of this short exchange, because, at bottom, Michal and David's comments here represent two different theological interpretations of events. Michal sees a man acting shamelessly for his own benefit, whereas David describes himself as a man whose success embodies God's will. Again, ambivalence rears its head. Which is it? Is it somehow both? The reason that this section is titled "David vs. God" is because David is trying to impose his theology on everyone around him and is meeting resistance.

Regardless, it's quite remarkable that the biblical text doesn't shy away from putting Michal's argument forward. Our instinct might be to take David's side—after all, he's the hero of the story. And yet, between the two, David will also turn out to be[33] the more morally compromised character.

Chapter 6 concludes with a note that Michal never had any children. Since the text reminds us that Michal is Saul's daughter, the most plausible reason for her childlessness is because any male child of hers would be a potential rival to David's rule. You don't go out of your way to eliminate a family only to bring it back to life. But apart from this political motivation, it stands to reason that their mutual distaste was not an aid to pregnancy.

God

After not hearing much from God during David's rise to power, we get one of God's longest speeches in these two books, delivered by the prophet Nathan to David. While the story of David and Goliath is one of the most popular literary passages in the Hebrew Bible, 2 Samuel 7 and the so-called "Davidic promise" or "Davidic covenant" is one of the most popular theological passages. Known by both Jewish and Christian communities as a passage of messianic significance, the theology of the chapter shapes what several religious communities think of God's future designs for humanity. But the chapter is not entirely positive for David, and some ambiguities and incongruities haunt the story.

The chapter begins with David settled into his home in his new capital of Jerusalem, and the text informs us that God gave David rest from his enemies (7:1b). This is a weird thing to say, considering that

---

[33] If he's not already.

David will fight the Philistines, Moabites, Arameans, and Edomites in the very next chapter and that the rest of 2 Samuel will be full of wars, against both foreign and domestic enemies. It's also a weird thing to say because v. 11 will describe David's "rest" as something yet to be given. This strangeness is likely why the line about God having given David rest is left out in 1 Chronicles 17:1, which parallels this verse. 1 and 2 Chronicles were written later, centuries later, and this strangeness didn't make sense to those authors either.

David complains to the prophet Nathan that he has a beautiful house, but God is still living in a tent, by which he means the ark is housed in a tent (7:3). David wants to be the one to build a grand temple for God instead. Aside from the social prestige of completing the project, it would secure Jerusalem as the permanent religious capital of the kingdom and require all his subjects in far-flung northern Israel to pilgrimage down to Jerusalem if they wanted to sacrifice in the presence of God. Nathan initially seems open to the idea (7:3), but God appears to Nathan in a dream that night and gives him a message to deliver to David (7:4). A big part of that message is a strongly worded "no thanks" to the temple idea.

Nathan says that God has not lived in a permanent house since bringing the people of Israel up out of Egypt and has never asked anyone to build one (7:5–7). Like buying your spouse a kitchen appliance they never asked for, David's desire to build a temple seems out of touch. Oops. This message is a powerful interpretive key for 1 and 2 Samuel because it answers an earlier question we had about whether or not David and God's will are identical. No, they're evidently not. And this interpretive key allows us to go back to texts where God responds with silence to David's morally suspect choices and know that these choices are not necessarily God's will at all.

Despite David's theological lapse, God is willing to give him a hell[34] of a concession prize. Playing on the theme of providing a home, God says that, through David, Israel will have a home where they won't

---

[34] Sorry, "heck."

be oppressed (7:8–11). God adds that David too will have a house (7:11b), not in a literal sense but in the sense of an enduring dynasty, and David's son will be the one who builds the temple (7:23a).

It's initially unclear why God wouldn't be willing to have a temple during David's time, but would be willing in the generation after. In 1 Kings 5:3, Solomon himself suggests that David was too busy fighting his enemies to build the temple himself, but this is another statement at odds with the idea that God gave David rest. Both 1 Chronicles 22:8 and 28:3 add that David was disqualified from building the temple because he shed too much blood. If the writers of 2 Samuel 7 knew either of these reasons, it's strange that they would appeal to God's tradition of being unhoused instead.

In the short term, the theology of chapter 7 shifts ancient Israel's self-conception: they go from being a people with a collective covenantal relationship with a God whose presence moves around, to being a people ruled by a king who has an individual covenantal relationship with a God whose presence is settled in a single place. The later histories we find in 1 and 2 Kings, and 1 and 2 Chronicles, will treat Davidic kings and the temple as the beating heart of the nation. In later prophetic texts, David's name becomes synonymous with the monarchy, Israel's political sovereignty, and the ideal relationship between God and humanity.

Because David's line is said to be permanent in 7:13b, 15–16, the theology of this chapter becomes the basis of several religions' messianic hopes. If a descendant of David is meant to be on the throne in Jerusalem literally forever, then in any period where there is no such descendant on the throne, there would be a reason for an ancient audience to hope and pray that God will intervene in history to make it so.

When Israel and Judah are dominated by a series of increasingly oppressive empires, their people will look back to David through a nostalgic lens and look forward to a Davidic savior who can return them to better times. When imperial oppression gets really bad and the Jewish people start writing apocalyptic literature about God tearing down empires, judging the dead, defeating evil itself, and remaking the world in a more perfect form, these hopes combine with the hopes of a future Davidic king to create the kind of expectations early Christians believed were fulfilled in Jesus.[35]

Because I said I would in the introduction, I have to talk about God and fatherhood in chapter 7. Verses 14 and 15 have one of the most straightforward affirmations of the fatherhood of God in the Hebrew Bible/Old Testament. The text says,

> I will be a father to him, and he shall be a son to me. When he commits iniquity, I will punish him with a rod such as mortals use, with blows inflicted by human beings. But I will not take my steadfast love from him, as I took it from Saul, whom I put away from before you. (2 Samuel 7:14–15)

This is very different from the kind of Mosaic covenants seen in the Pentateuch. There, the people of Israel are to be a nation of priests (Exodus 19:6) and holy like God is holy (Leviticus 11:44). That is to say, as part of the covenant, the human becomes more divine, taking on the attributes of God. But here, it's the opposite. As part of this covenant, the divine becomes more human, with God taking on the attributes of a hypothetical father.

I say hypothetical because the attributes described are...not great? Mid at best? Not necessarily representative of fatherhood? Not even that great in the ancient context in which these stories are set?

The text says God will punish David's descendents, but God will still love those descendents. To simplify: painful punishments but love regardless. That's a pretty low and unsatisfying bar for a parent in general and a father in particular. Even if we were to restrict our ideas to what a parent does in response to a child's misbehavior, there's no positive reinforcement, creation of a safe environment, modeling of good

---

[35] If you're interested in learning more about apocalyptic literature, you should check out Robyn J. Whitaker's book for The Bible for Normal People: *Revelation for Normal People: A Guide to the Strangest and Most Dangerous Book in the Bible* (Harleysville, PA: Bible for Normal People, 2023).

behavior, consistent communication, or guided coping for emotional competence. Here, it's just "make them suffer when they do something wrong, and keep loving them." We should dare to want more out of fathers, both human and divine.

This antagonistic, almost police-like conception of fatherhood leaves a lot to be desired, and it almost inevitably pits children against their fathers, another reason why this section is called "David vs. God." Whatever you think of this kind of fatherhood, it's worth keeping in mind because, in the next section, we will begin to look at David as a father.

David

The remainder of chapter 7 is a prayer by David, thanking God for the establishment of his dynasty. Chapter 8 sees David fighting wars against every bordering nation that lies north, south, east, and west; he is expanding his territory, killing thousands, and collecting tribute. God appears briefly in a reminder by the narrator that God gives David all these victories (8:14b). Their wills appear to have lined up again.

A brief note at the end of the chapter tells us about some of David's political appointments, a few of which are significant. Joab is officially put in command of the army (8:16), despite David's earlier public complaints about how he is uncontrollably violent. Then, verse 17 mentions the priest "Ahimelech son of Abiathar." This should actually be the other way around. Abiathar is the son of Ahimelech. Ahimelech was the priest David convinced to give him supplies at Nob (1 Samuel 21:1–9) when he was on the run from Saul and whom Saul later had executed (1 Samuel 22:11–19). Abiathar is Ahimelech's son who escaped the massacre (1 Samuel 22:20–23) and went to join up with David. Lastly, we're told that a man named Benaiah was put in charge of the Cherethites and Pelethites, who are essentially units of mercenary Philistine special forces.

Although it won't be relevant for a while, all three men—Joab, Abiathar, and Benaiah—will play significant roles in the events surrounding David's death and the succession of the throne to his son Solomon.

Chapter 9 then turns to a story of Mephibosheth, the physically disabled son of Jonathan, and Ziba, a steward of what remains of Saul's household. For Jonathan's sake (9:1), David takes in Mephibosheth, showing him the "kindness of God" (9:3) by allowing him to eat at his table (9:13). "Eat at his table" is more than just a meal; it's providing economic security for someone and sheltering them. Mephibosheth's disability (9:3) is the likely reason why David wouldn't be concerned with him posing as a rival to his power. Rather, David is asserting a kind of social power over Mephibosheth by providing for him. This scene harkens back to David and Jonathan's oaths to show kindness between their descendants forever (1 Samuel 20:42) and David's oath to Saul that he would not permanently cut off Saul's line (1 Samuel 24:21–22).

David closes 2 Samuel 9 at the height of his power: the remainder of Saul's household has been dealt with in one form or another; every possible foreign enemy is in submission; his own political and religious capital have been established; and God has promised him a never-ending dynasty. But 2 Samuel has twenty-four chapters, and David does not die for two more chapters beyond that. What could possibly fill this space, then?

David is going to learn that, when you're at the top, the only place you can go is down.

CHAPTER FOUR

David's Fall

Bathsheba vs. David (2 Samuel 10–12)

David goes to war with the Ammonites and confronts the Aramean mercenaries they have hired. Due to Joab's tactical abilities, the Israelite army is able to prevail against the mercenaries, but the siege of the Ammonites is protracted. David stays in Jerusalem during these battles, and, upon seeing Bathsheba bathing from the heights of his palace, orders her to his home and rapes her.

In an effort to cover up his role in Bathsheba's resulting pregnancy, David orders Uriah, one his elite soldiers and Bathsheba's husband, to return home and sleep with his wife. Uriah's honor prevents him from doing so while the Israelite army is still in the field. David then orders Joab to have Uriah killed in battle by abandoning him on the front line. After Uriah's death, David marries Bathsheba.

But the prophet Nathan discovers David's adulterous plot and uses a hypothetical scenario to get David to condemn himself, resulting in God placing something like a curse on David's reign. The child of David's rape dies, his son Solomon is born to Bathsheba, and Joab and David finish off the Ammonites together.

Bathsheba

In 2 Samuel 10, we read of David's war against the Ammonites, an ethnic group positioned just beyond the northeast side of his territory. Much of the chapter repeats elements of what we heard in chapter 8 about his conflict with the Arameans, who get involved when the Ammonites hire them as mercenaries. Frankly, the material is boring and redundant and I won't be talking about it.[1]

The important takeaway point from chapter 10 is that the siege against the Ammonites is protracted. Joab is able to defeat the Aramean mercenaries rather easily (10:9–14), but the fighting against the Ammonites in their capital of Rabbah appears to take two years, depending on how you read the story. It's during the extended siege that the stories in chapters 11 and 12 are set. And it's during this siege that we're introduced to the character of Bathsheba.

The beginning of chapter 11 tells us that David is staying in Jerusalem while Joab handles the siege against the Ammonites (11:1). This is unusual, both for David in particular and for kings more generally. David is famous for being a commander of military men, for winning unwinnable battles (like against Goliath), and for being a successful mercenary. For him to sit in his palace while Joab and the army are out fighting is a major change for his character and an early indication that he's in a period of decline.

Staying home is also unusual for kings in general; at the very least, they will condescend to take the field in a reserve position surrounded by a large personal guard for protection. A king's presence on the battlefield is expected, and a king's absence is suspicious if not outright shameful. Not even Saul stayed home after being told by the ghost of Samuel [2] that he'd die in battle. If Saul could get out there, then what does it say that David can't?

---

[1] So there.

[2] The ghost of Samuel past? Or the ghost of Samuel future? I'm not sure.

One night, David takes a stroll on the roof of his palace overlooking the city, and he looks down into the central courtyard of a beautiful woman's home while she is bathing. It's possible this is a routine bath or that it's a ritual bath at the end of her period (11:2). If the latter, this act tells us that she's a pious woman, fulfilling her obligations to maintain ritual purity. Either way, David sends people to find out who she is and learns that she's Bathsheba, daughter of Eliam and wife of Uriah (11:3).

What the text doesn't explicitly say, but we can infer from what we gather elsewhere, is that David knows exactly who Bathsheba is. It's virtually impossible for them to not have met before. Eliam, Bathsheba's father, and Uriah, Bathsheba's husband, are both one of David's "thirty"—his most elite soldiers and personal guard (2 Samuel 23:34b, 39). Eliam is also the son of Ahithophel, one of David's most trusted advisors, who we will meet in a few chapters. David will have hosted Bathsheba at any number of social and religious gatherings as a woman closely associated with his household. Bathsheba is not a random woman to David, but a close associate.

Despite this, when David learns who Bathsheba is, he has her brought to his palace, and he rapes her (11:4). "Rape" might not be the word you're expecting to see here, or it may be a word you're uncomfortable seeing here, and that's understandable. We can make allowances for a lot of David's behavior. Rape would be a bridge too far for many people, but it's the appropriate term here even if that's not apparent in the wording. The original Hebrew simply says David "lay with" her, but that's not definitive since biblical Hebrew has no specific word for either "sex" or "rape," just a variety of euphemisms. "Rape" is apparent from the context. Bathsheba is plucked from the privacy of her own home in the midst of a religious ritual, in a situation where all the power is on David's side, and she can't say no without catastrophic consequences. That's rape. And given David's tendency to forcibly take women from their husbands, rape is not inconsistent with David's character.

If this were a purely academic commentary, I'd probably leave this next part out. But you chose to buy this book, and it comes with the soapboxes I stand on.

There are people who will try to blame Bathsheba for what David does to her. There are people who will say that Bathsheba seduces David somehow, and that this was all part of some plan on her part to end up as queen. These ideas should be resisted vehemently. They have no basis in the text, and every second we spend entertaining them provides cover for people who make similar excuses on behalf of rapists today.

Sometime later, Bathsheba sends word to David that she's pregnant (11:5). David calls Uriah back from the siege of Rabah, and between verses 6 and 13, he attempts to get Uriah to go home to Bathsheba and "wash his feet" (again, a euphemism for sex) in the hopes of covering up his own role in the pregnancy. But Uriah is a man of honor and can't bear to go home while his comrades are deployed (11:11). So David sends Uriah back to the front lines carrying a message for Joab to have Uriah abandoned in the midst of heavy fighting (11:14–15). Joab carries out this order, and Uriah is killed (11:16–17).

When Bathsheba hears that Uriah is dead, she grieves for him (11:26). She had probably been waiting fearfully for the news ever since she told David she was pregnant, knowing what kind of man David was. When Bathsheba's period of grieving is over, David moves her into his palace, and she remains there until his death. We will hear from Bathsheba again, at the end of David's life, where she plays a part in the drama surrounding the succession. There, unlike here, she does have a small measure of a voice.

The story of David and Bathsheba is another interpretive key that we can apply in retrospect to things we've already read. If, in the section discussing David and Abigail, you thought I was crazy for suggesting that David engineered Nabal's death through Abigail, well, here you go. David is happy to knowingly rape the wives of his close associates and murder them in order to avoid responsibility. Now the idea of David having Nabal killed off doesn't seem so implausible. Perhaps you thought it was silly to suggest that David was behind Ishbaal's death, or Abner's death, or Saul's death. Now, that seems like nothing in comparison to what's happening here.

David

God is not happy with David (11:27b). In one of the clearest examples of the schism between God and David's will, God sends the prophet Nathan to tell David a story about a terrible injustice in the land: a wealthy man has stolen the prized possession of a poor man. David flies into a rage, demanding the man in question pay back fourfold what he took (12:1–6), whereupon Nathan reveals that David himself is the man. Nathan then unloads a series of punishments on David, including civil war (12:10–11a), the public rape of the women of his household (12:11b–12), and the death of his child by Bathsheba (12:14).

These punishments are quite harsh; but at the same time, they're not really punishments that David himself has to bear. If this is God acting in the capacity of a father who distributes punishments, it's a bit of a misfire, as these punishments do a better job of punishing the people around David than they do punishing David himself. Even within the narrow conception of a father as a punishing figure, where presumably a good father punishes justly and a bad father punishes unjustly, God comes off as a bad father.

After the death of David and Bathsheba's baby, David "comforts" Bathsheba, and she conceives a second time and gives birth to Solomon (12:24). The chapter ends with Joab breaking Rabah's defenses (12:26) and sending for David so he can come and take credit for the win (12:28). It's a subtle reminder that David's best days are behind him.

Tamar vs. Amnon (2 Samuel 13–14)

David's oldest son Amnon, with encouragement from his friend, rapes his half-sister Tamar. Two years later, Absalom, Tamar's other brother, gets revenge on her behalf by having Amnon killed at a feast while he's drunk. Absalom flees to his mother's homeland, outside David's territory, putting the anticipated line of succession in trouble. Joab then conspires with a wise woman to get Absalom and David to reconcile, at which point Absalom returns to Jerusalem.

Tamar

Back in 2 Samuel 3:1–5, in a section I skipped because no one cares about genealogies,[3] we were told about David's first round of sons. We're given the name of one son by each of David's then six wives (before the addition of Michal and Bathsheba). On that list was David's oldest son and heir apparent, Amnon, son of Ahinoam.[4] But also on that list was Absalom, son of Maacah, who was the daughter of the king of Geshur. Geshur is a territory northeast of Israel, but the *Geshurites* are a people southwest of Israel whom David raided during his time as a Philistine mercenary (1 Samuel 27:8). The latter is a more plausible explanation for Maacah's origins, as David tends to "collect" wives from places where he is otherwise fighting.

Absalom has a sister called Tamar, and in the opening verse of chapter 13, we're told that Amnon "loves" her (13:1). This word needs to be put in several side-eye air quotes, because although it's an accurate rendering of the Hebrew, it's not an accurate description of Amnon's actual feelings, as we will shortly see.

Amnon is complaining about the fact that he can't get with his half-sister to his friend Jonadab, who happens to be one of David's elite soldiers (2 Samuel 21:21). So Jonadab, being "very wise"[5] (13:3), concocts a plan and tells Amnon to fake being sick so Tamar will come to his room to take care of him (13:4–8). Amnon follows his friend's advice and asks David to send Tamar to him. When she arrives, he

---

[3] You didn't even notice, did you? DID YOU?
[4] The lady who either was, or happened to have the same name as, one of Saul's wives. Since I'm all about that drama, I choose the first.
[5] Again, with the side-eye quotations.

orders everyone else out of the room and tells her to sleep with him (13:9–11).

While many women are sexually assaulted in the Bible, Tamar is one of the few whose voice of resistance is recorded in the narrative. Tamar attempts three arguments to dissuade Amnon: (1) rape isn't something Israelites do (13:12); (2) she wouldn't be able to hide her pregnancy (13:13a); and (3) Amnon could just ask David for her hand in marriage if he wanted her (13:13b).

The arguments are good. Contra Jonadab, Tamar's wisdom should be recognized. Her first argument appeals to cultural consensus, something we earlier saw Amnon wrestling with as he fretted about not being able to touch her (13:2). Tamar is insightful for being able to guess what kind of reasoning Amnon might be sensitive to.

Her second argument appeals to consequences, and if Amnon were thinking rationally, it probably would have worked. If her pregnancy became public and Amnon was discovered as the father, then Amnon could face serious consequences because he would have deprived David of the opportunity to arrange a politically beneficial marriage for her.

Her third argument is clever as well. If Amnon genuinely loved Tamar as the text claims, then there wasn't anything stopping him from pursuing a legitimate marriage with her. And since ancient marriage presumes sexual access, he could have sex with her that way. There are other marriages to half-siblings in biblical texts, Abraham and Sarah being the most famous (Genesis 20:21), though it's difficult to know whether David would approve of the practice. Regardless, if Amnon had agreed, it would have diffused the immediate situation and given her a chance to escape.

There is a law in Leviticus 18:11 that explicitly prohibits sex between half-siblings like this, but this story in 2 Samuel is almost certainly older than that law, and it's difficult to know whether any of those laws were ever rigorously followed. Tamar seems to think that marriage is possible between them, and that's what matters most.

Unfortunately, Amnon is David's son, and the apple hasn't fallen far from the tree. Amnon is not deterred, and he rapes Tamar.

Immediately after, Amnon undergoes a dramatic reversal of feeling and comes to hate Tamar more than he "loved" her (13:15). He orders her to leave, and Tamar points out that this would be an even greater violation than the first, since cultural convention would not allow her to marry anyone else (13:16). But again, Amnon can't be persuaded, and he forces her out of his house.

It's around this time that David hears what happened (13:21). His reaction is thoroughly disappointing. He gets mad. That's it. Nothing else. He doesn't condemn Amnon. He doesn't comfort Tamar. He doesn't track down Jonadab and have him executed for plotting the rape of his daughter. He just gets mad.

And the fact that he just gets mad is a perfect explanation for how this all could have happened to begin with. David is an absentee father, so disconnected from the lives of his children that even when one assaults another, he can't bring himself to do more than be angry. This even fails to live up to the low bar of fatherhood set by God in the Davidic promise back in chapter 7. David can't even meaningfully punish his child. Eli had the same problem back in 1 Samuel 2:23–25.

But it fails a more realistic standard as well. David has obviously failed to model positive behavior for Amnon. David has raped women. He's almost famous for doing it and getting away with it, so it's little surprise that his son follows suit. David has also failed to surround himself and his children with good people, as Amnon is only able to rape Tamar because of the advice of one of David's closest soldiers. And David has further failed to comfort his daughter in any way. David never says a word to Tamar in the Bible.

That's four parenting failures, and while that by itself could be enough to conclude that David is a bad father, we've only begun to scratch the surface of the consequences his failures bring about.

After the assault, Absalom takes Tamar into his home, where she lives out the rest of her life as a destitute woman (13:20). Absalom intuits what has happened to Tamar without her having to say, which implies that Amnon's feelings for Tamar were known, at least within David's immediate circle. Absalom attempts to comfort his sister, but he also tells her to keep quiet. Absalom has a plan, and he bides his time for two years. Eventually he persuades David to let Amnon come with him to a sheep shearing festival, and when Amnon is good and truly drunk during a feast, Absolom's men ambush and assassinate him (13:23–29). There is irony and/or a kind of poetic justice here. Amnon had David send his victim to him. Absalom had David send his victim to him. Tamar was placed in a position where she could not resist. Amnon, via alcohol, is also placed in a position where he could not resist.

Afterwards, Absalom flees to his mother's people in Geshur and spends three years there (13:38). Interestingly, the one character who is consoled in this chapter is David, concerning the death of Amnon (13:39), which is like the least sad thing that happens here. Apparently, David is able to get over Amnon dying [6] and yearns to be reunited with Absalom. Little does David know that their reunion will be a precursor to civil war.

Joab

Without any battles to fight in these chapters, Joab has different work to do. For better or worse,[7] Absalom is now the oldest son of David and heir to the throne. But Absalom has fled into self-imposed exile in a foreign land to avoid the consequences of murdering his brother. As is often the case, David has made a mess, and Joab is left to clean it up.

Joab finds an unnamed wise woman from Tekoa (14:1–2), a city south of Jerusalem, and he tells her to go before David and tell him a story. Like the prophet Nathan's story of a wealthy man stealing a prized possession from a poor man, the wise woman's story is a fiction meant to indict David by analogy.

With a hefty bit of flattery thrown in, the wise woman tells a story of two quarreling brothers. One brother kills the other and then flees to

---

[6] Me too, tbh.

[7] The answer is worse.

avoid retribution. The wise woman begs to have the living brother pardoned so that their father's line can continue (14:3–11). David agrees, and the wise woman points out that the situation with Absalom is the same. He ought to be pardoned too. David is smart enough to figure out that Joab put the wise woman up to the story (14:18–20), but he still agrees to bring Absalom home (14:24), and after some time, David and Absalom reconcile (14:33).

But the most important takeaway[8] for the development of Joab's character is his motivation for helping David and Absalom reconcile. The first verse of the chapter tells us Joab "knew that the heart of the king was on Absalom." Joab was sensitive to David's emotions, and, seeing his longtime friend/confidante in pain, he took steps to fix it.

Joab has no practical reason to reconcile David and Absalom. It's of no political or military benefit to him. If Absalom simply stayed in exile forever or vanished from the face of the earth, they'd find a new heir. David isn't short on sons. But Joab helps David because Joab is the kind of man who helps his friend. I think that's important to establish now, because when that friendship is put under enormous pressure in the chapters to come, we should remember what it was before.

David vs. Absalom (2 Samuel 15–20)

Absalom wins the hearts of the people of Israel through grandstanding and politicking, then he has himself declared king at Hebron, just like his father before him. David flees Jerusalem as Absalom's army approaches, but he is able to leave spies behind in the city. Under advice from Ahithophel, David's former advisor, Absalom rapes the women in David's harem in full view of everyone in Jerusalem as a way of establishing himself as king.

But David's spies are able to give bad military advice to Absalom and to leak Absalom's movements to David. David rallies in northern

---

[8] Imho.

Israel and then engages Absalom's army when they pursue him, though he warns his commanders to spare Absalom's life. Under Joab's command, Absalom's army is slaughtered, and Joab kills Absalom. When David receives news of Absalom's death, he's devastated and cries publicly, shaming the soldiers who fought to secure his victory. Joab calls out David for his lack of appreciation, and David returns to Jerusalem. But he returns to a far less stable kingdom than he left.

Absalom

Back when David was first introduced, the narrator noted how beautiful he was (1 Samuel 16:12). A similar note is given in 2 Samuel 14:25–26, where Absalom is described as being without blemish and having especially long hair. These descriptions weren't relevant before, but they are now. Like his father, Absalom is attractive to many people he interacts with; he's also willing to kill (i.e., his older brother) and has ambitions for the throne. It's Absalom's similarities to his father that foreshadow the events of chapters 15–19.

Absalom begins by getting himself a chariot and horses, which are associated with the kingship in ancient Israel. Back in 1 Samuel 8:11, Samuel had told the Israelites that a king would get horses, a chariot, and young men to run alongside it, exactly as Absalom does. Deuteronomy 17:16 also warns against a king acquiring too many horses. What's more, Absalom starts hearing people's cases (15:2–6), which is a task the king is supposed to perform, and he loudly proclaims that he would be great at doing a king's job. He does this all while gladhanding anyone who comes by, building up his public reputation.

After four years of this, Absalom sends secret messengers throughout Israel's territories announcing that he will be named king. He also conspires with David's advisor Ahithophel and gets David's permission to travel to Hebron (where David himself was first anointed) with several hundred men by his side (15:7–12).

I think it speaks to David's declining power that Absalom is able to engineer a coup right under his nose with so little effort. It probably also hints at a blind spot David has with respect to Absalom. David doesn't see the coup coming because he doesn't want to see the coup coming. Whatever the case might be, Absalom's armies come rolling into Jerusalem and those loyal to David flee.

When Absalom enters Jerusalem, he asks Ahithophel what he should do, probably by way of cementing his power over the capital (16:20). Ahithophel gives Absalom the despicable advice of publicly raping the women in David's harem whom he had left behind (16:21)—ten concubines in total (15:16)—so that everyone in Jerusalem will know that he has made David his enemy. This is an extreme example of what we've seen before, like with Abner and Saul's concubine, where ambitious men try to have sex with the women of past kings in order to occupy that king's position.

It is also a disturbing fulfillment of the prophecy announced by Nathan as a consequence of David's rape of Bathsheba. What David did in secret, God is going to do to him in public (12:12). David is guilty of rape in private, so David's concubines are raped in public. Again, we should note that the concubines themselves are entirely innocent, but they are bearing the burden of David's consequences. It's also an indirect act of revenge if we remember that Ahithophel is Bathsheba's grandfather. Ahithophel has personal reasons to see David suffer, although, again, it's his concubines who actually suffer.

Next, Ahithophel advises that Absalom immediately pursue David's fleeing forces and attack him while he is at his most discouraged (17:1–4). But another advisor named Hushai, who is actually a spy for David, advises that Absalom hold off, gather an army from all Israel, and lead the battle himself against David (17:5–14). Absalom decides to go with this course of action, probably because it seems both safer and more glorious, and that gives time for Hushai to send word to David about Absalom's plans. When Ahithophel sees his advice being ignored, he commits suicide (17:23), likely knowing that David will win and come in search of his traitorous advisor.

And David does win. Absalom's army, as large as it is, is annihilated by David's more experienced soldiers. Absalom himself flees on his mule, and his hair gets stuck in the branches of an oak tree (18:9). His mule runs off, leaving him hanging by his hair. Joab finds him in the tree, helpless. Despite having been ordered by David to deal gently with Absalom (18:5), Joab shows him no mercy. While Absalom is held by his long and beautiful hair, Joab pierces him with spears, a gruesome but ironic way for a mass rapist to die.

Absalom is the perfect foil for David because he is so much like him. Everything that David aspired to do and succeeded at, Absalom tried to do and failed. Every evil David did along the way, Absalom did and then some. Like father, like son, Absalom is David's greatest mistake. The only real difference between them is that David (sometimes) has God on his side to help him win, and Absalom does not.

David

David's story in this section is one of retreat, concession, and despair. We hear nothing from David until half way through chapter 15, where a messenger has to deliver the news of Absalom's coup and the impending capture of Jerusalem by his forces (15:13). An engaged, conscientious, or even mildly aware parent could not have been caught off guard by the public, years-long strides Absalom was making toward the throne. Even a terrible parent who was nevertheless a shrewd and effective ruler should have seen this coming.

The narrative of David's flight is prolonged and awkwardly paced, with constant descriptions of people he meets and stops he makes along the way. David initially flees with all of his officials and household, save for the ten concubines he leaves behind (15:14–16). No reason is given for why these women have to stay, and David must have known that in staying, they were placed in a dangerous situation. Then we're told he is also leaving with his Philistine mercenaries: the Cherethites, Pelethites, and hundreds of additional Gittites (15:18–23).

Abiathar the priest, who had been with David since his outlaw days, tries to bring the ark of the covenant on the run with David, but David declines. Outside the city, David hears that Ahithophel has betrayed him and sided with Absalom, and David prays that God will frustrate the advice Ahithophel gives (15:31), which does eventually happen. Then David meets a man named Hushai, whom he sends back to the city along with Abiathar to be spies for him (15:33–37). This, too, turns out to be a prudent move.

David then meets Ziba, the steward of Saul's physically disabled grandson, Mephibosheth, whom he had taken in. Ziba says that Saul's son has betrayed him in expectation of being restored to the throne by Absalom (16:1–3). David rewards Ziba with all of Mephibosheth's possessions (16:4), but it's possible Ziba was lying for exactly that purpose, as once the civil war is over, Mephibosheth says as much (19:24–30).

A final meeting leads to a poignant moment for David. A man named Shimei, who was a member of Saul's household, taunts David as he flees Jerusalem, insulting him and throwing rocks at him.[9] Abisahi, Joab's brother, offers to relieve the man of his head, but David has an introspective moment instead (16:11). If even his son wants to kill him, then how much more so a man with legitimate grievances? This moment of earnest wrestling with his own actions sounds similar to moments during Saul's reign when he was confronted by Jonathan or David and admitted his failures.

Eventually David reaches the far northeastern fortress city of Mahanaim. David has run as far as he can go from Jerusalem. The Ammonites, to whom Joab laid siege for two years in chapters 10–12, are now under new leadership, and they send substantial provisions for David and his army (17:27–29). This allows David to rally and organize his army (18:1–2). David's soldiers do not allow him to participate in the battle (18:3–4). This is a smart, tactical decision, since Absalom is really hunting David and not his army. David then warns his commanders, Joab included, to treat Absalom gently in the battle to come (18:5).

David's unique affection for Absalom has come up several times in instances where he is on the verge of losing him. Unfortunately, that unique affection never seemed to manifest in Absalom's life on any

---

[9] Bro wants to die.

occasion where it would have improved his character or their relationship as father and son. After all, as David himself admits, Absalom is
actively trying to kill him.

Joab

While Joab may have been involved in any number of ways in the
escape from Jerusalem and the muster of David's army in Mahanaim,
we don't actually hear from Joab until the stage is set for the battle with
Absalom. Joab does what he does best, and crushes Absalom's army.
Joab gets word from a random soldier that Absalom is caught in a tree
and hanging from his hair, and he finds it distasteful that the man
didn't just kill Absalom right there (18:10–13). So Joab himself kills
Absalom (18:14) in blatant violation of David's wishes.

It's the ease with which he kills Absalom that justifies, in retrospect, the idea that Joab helped reconcile Absalom and David purely
out of devotion to his friend. Clearly, Joab has no compunction about
living without Absalom.

So why kill him now when David wants him kept alive? It might
be for purely pragmatic reasons; after all, Joab is essentially responsible
for the defense of David's kingdom, and Absalom almost destroyed it.
It might also be because Joab thinks it's genuinely in his friend's best
interest. David's blindness to Absalom clearly has a weakening effect on
him. The loss of one evil man, son or not, is a small price to pay to try
to get David's head back in the game.

When David gets news of Absalom's death, he is utterly inconsol-
able (18:33–19:2), which ruins the morale of David's army who had
fought so hard for him after a desperate flight from home (19:3–4).
Joab hits David with some hard truths, which are worth quoting in
full:

> Today you have covered with shame the faces of all your officers
> who have saved your life today, and the lives of your sons and your
> daughters, and the lives of your wives and your concubines, for

love of those who hate you and for hatred of those who love you. You have made it clear today that commanders and officers are nothing to you, for I perceive that, if Absalom were alive and all of us were dead today, then you would be pleased. (2 Samuel 19:5–6, NRSVue).

Not a single lie was told. David, the man who needed consolation after his daughter was raped when he himself gave none, has utterly neglected the value of all the people upon whom his life and his power depend.

David didn't fight, his soldiers did. His sons and daughters have suffered poor parenting, assault, humiliation, and death without a word from him. His wives have suffered from his rapacious habits. His concubines have suffered the divinely ordained consequences of those habits at the hands of his son. Those who are loyal to David receive no love at all, but Absalom, who has betrayed him, receives all the belated love in the world. David's confusion of love and hatred mirrors his son Amnon's confusion of the same feelings, just on a kingdom's scale. Joab's final indictment rings true. It does seem that David would prefer a living Absalom and a dead everyone else.

Joab is obviously speaking from a personal perspective on this issue. He has been loyal to his friend and uncle since their outlaw days on the run from Saul. For every victory the biblical author wants to attribute to God, there is Joab, winning the battles on the ground. It's very reasonable to wonder how far David might have gone without Joab. And yet, when has David ever shown Joab the love Joab has shown for him? What thing has David done for Joab that compares to the things Joab has done for him? Has David ever done anything for Joab? This is the tragic climax of Joab and David's relationship.

David listens to Joab, stops his public weeping, and makes a more dignified appearance before his subjects to reassure them (19:8). But the relationship between David and Joab is never the same.

The aftermath of the battle is politically complicated. Absalom had a special appeal for the people of northern Israel. Absalom was the most beautiful in "all Israel" (14:25); he stole the hearts of all the people of Israel (15:6) and sent messengers throughout "all the tribes of Israel" before declaring himself king (15:10). He arrived in Jerusalem for his coup with "all the men of Israel" (16:15), and it's "the men of Israel" (18:7) who were defeated by Joab in battle. While the term "Israel" can refer to all twelve tribes in the whole region of Canaan, later, after the death of Solomon, it will refer to the ten northern tribes who break away from Judah and form a separate kingdom (1 Kings 12). In 2 Samuel 19:9–15, those tensions are already evident.

In order to reunify the whole of Israel after nearly losing his kingship, David appoints Amasa as commander over the army in place of Joab (19:13). Amasa had been Absalom's short-lived commander, so his appointment is likely a concession to northern Israelites who supported Absalom's rebellion.

Chapter 19 ends with another flare-up of tensions between the north and the south (19:41–42). It seems that, although the civil war was traumatic for David and his army, some people in northern Israel actually appreciated David's stay in Mahanaim in the north, and they see his return to Jerusalem in the south as a loss. The north believes the south is prejudicial and unreasonable because, while they have ten shares in David (ten tribes), the south only has two (19:43).

No sooner has the first civil war been resolved than a second begins in chapter 20. A man named Sheba capitalizes on the tensions between Israel in the north and Judah in the south, and he calls on northerners to break away from David (20:1). Amasa is sent to rally the army as Joab and David's Philistine special forces go off in pursuit of Sheba (20:4–7). But Joab, not the kind of man to be demoted, murders Amasa and reclaims his place as commander of the army (20:8–10). Joab and the army then corner Sheba on the far northern edge of Israel in a city called Beth-Maacah, and they begin a siege (20:14–15). But a wise woman of the city parlays with Joab, and after finding out he's only interested in Sheba, she has Sheba's head cut off (20:16–22). With the usurper dead, Joab returns to Jerusalem.

David vs. Himself (2 Samuel 21–24)

The last four chapters of 2 Samuel contain supplemental materials and stories that aren't necessarily in chronological order. After a famine strikes the land, David satisfies the bloodguilt of Saul's household by turning over seven of Saul's sons to the Gibeonites for execution. The names and great deeds of David's elite soldiers are recorded, along with his last words and a final prayer.

The final chapter tells a story of David taking a census of the people of Israel. This angers God, and David must choose his punishment. He chooses a plague, and tens of thousands die as a result. Just when the plague is about to consume Jerusalem, David takes responsibility, and the plague is averted.

David

The primary story of David's rise and fall concluded with 2 Samuel 20. The final chapters of 2 Samuel are made up of three kinds of material: (1) secondary narratives out of chronological order that might be either too embarrassing or written too late to be included elsewhere; (2) lists of David's elite soldiers and their deeds; and (3) records of David's final words.

Chapter 21 opens with the first kind of material and is probably most associated with 2 Samuel 9, since it deals with David's treatment of Saul's remaining household and the survival of Mephibosheth. We're told that there was a famine in the land, and through divination, David discovers the cause is the bloodguilt of Saul's house in light of their treatment of the Gibeonites (21:1). The Gibeonites were a Canaanite group from Joshua 9, who tricked Joshua into making a treaty with them instead of being exterminated. There is no story of Saul's mistreatment of the Gibeonites, so it seems that some tradition is missing.

The Gibeonites demand that seven of Saul's sons be given to them for execution to clear Israel and David of the bloodguilt, and David complies (21:6). Two of the sons handed over are children of Rizpah,

Saul's concubine, whom Abner had raped back in 2 Samuel 3 as a way of posturing for the throne in place of Ishbaal.

Rizpah is the heart of this short and brutal story. For months, she stands vigil over the bodies of her children (21:10). This isn't something she could accomplish on her own. No doubt people, other women most likely, brought her food and water, kept watch over her children's bodies while she slept, and came to comfort and support her during these grueling months of public mourning. Her vigil prompts David to recover the bones of Saul and Jonathan and give them a more dignified burial. In case this point has not been made enough, *so often* in these stories it's women who function as objects to be used and abused by men in their plays for power. Despite this, the power of Rizpah's agency to move David (a man not normally moved by women) and move those who came to support her, should also be recognized.

Christian readers of the Hebrew Bible often look to find hints of Jesus in these historical characters, and because of the Davidic promise and the messianic expectations that come to be attached to it, David is a common character to be seen in this light. I would suggest instead that it is many of the women in these stories who, as Isaiah says, take up the pain of men and bear their suffering (53:4), who are pierced for and by men's transgressions (53:5), and who face an ignoble death despite their innocence (53:9). The narratives in 1 and 2 Samuel feature so many women of so many different ethnicities and social classes; yet these women are unified in their experience of suffering for the sins of the men around them.

Both 2 Samuel 21:15–22 and 23:8–39 describe the deeds of David's "mighty men," and many of these deeds refer to combat with the Philistines that happened early in David's career while he was still under Saul's employ. Interesting bits here include Elhanan's killing of Goliath (21:19), which contradicts the account of David killing him in 1 Samuel 16; the mention of Jonabad/Jonathan, the son of Shimei, who talked Amnon into raping Tamar (21:21); and the passing reference to Uriah the Hittite, who, as you'll recall, was married to Bathsheba and effectively murdered by David (23:39).

Interestingly, while both of Joab's brothers, Abishai (23:18) and Asahel (23:24), are featured on the list, Joab himself is not. Although David's elite soldiers are divided into "the three" and "the thirty," there are actually thirty-five names in most manuscripts and thirty-six in others, while 23:39 explicitly states there were thirty-seven in all. So perhaps Joab's presence is simply assumed.

In 2 Samuel 22:1–23:7, there are two poems accredited to David as his last words. The poem in chapter 22 is very similar to Psalm 18 and is a fairly conventional psalm of praise, where the speaker applauds a powerful and just God for intervening to save the speaker from their enemies. The poem in chapter 23 is much shorter and is centered around the justice of a king who rules in fear of God, perhaps reflecting an idealized portrait of David's reign.

Chapter 24 tells the book's final story, where David takes a census of the people of Israel and is punished for it. Like chapter 21, it's difficult to know when this story is set. It would make sense for David to take a census upon first rising to the throne of a united Israel and Judah, alongside his administrative appointments in chapter 8. It might also make sense if it had happened after the reunification of northern Israel and southern Judah following the civil wars with Absalom and Sheba in chapters 15–20, especially since those chapters explicitly separate Israel and Judah. We're going to presume that it's set around this latter time and that it therefore reflects one of the very last acts of David.

The story begins, awkwardly, with an angry God inciting David to take the census for which he's then punished (24:1). Since this is theologically problematic and contradicts the kind of fatherly relationship God committed to in 2 Samuel 7, 1 Chronicles 21:1 changes the story so that Satan incites David to take the census instead. As Joab explains, taking a census is a sin (1 Samuel 24:4), as the primary reasons for doing so would be related to the king's profit, e.g., taxation, corvee labor, and military conscription. But David insists and the census moves forward.

A big question is "why"? What motivation could David have for doing this? Apart from the notion that God/Satan made him do it, what human facts account for this? If we consider where we are in the narrative, I think the best answer is that David is having a last-minute, panicked search for a meaningful legacy.

David has lost three sons—Absalom, Amnon, and his infant child with Bathsheba. There is no apparent heir to the throne to continue with the everlasting covenant God promised him. Any successes David had as king were drastically undercut by the civil wars he had to fight and the tensions between northern Israel and Judah that resulted. For someone who had such a #blessed rise to power, what does he have to show for it now? Not much.

A census, though, might show in an abstract way that he's managed to father a large, prosperous, and semi-united kingdom. This kingdom itself becomes a substitute child, since his relationships with his actual children were so poor. He could console himself at the end of his life by believing "at least Israel is strong."

Joab returns with a number of 1.3 million able-bodied men who could fight (24:9). That's several times larger than the total population of this region at the time, but biblical numbers are often a little wonky.

No sooner has the census been completed than David is struck with a guilty conscience (24:10). God taps the prophet Gad to give David three choices of punishment for conducting the census: three years of famine; three months of David being pursued by his foes; or three days of pestilence in the land (24:11–14). David chooses pestilence, resulting in the deaths of 70,000 people.[10] Just when the angel of God who's dispensing the pestilence is about to destroy Jerusalem, David does something he's never done before: he takes responsibility for what he's done (24:16–17). The pestilence is then averted, because it was David and his choices that had caused it all along.

And so it is here, only at the very end of things, where David comes face to face with the true antagonist of the story: himself.

---

[10] Again, wonky.

Intermission

If you read the title page of this book, then you'll see it says "1 and 2 Samuel" on it. With the pestilence of 2 Samuel 24 ended and Jerusalem saved by David's piety, 2 Samuel is done. You might reasonably expect this book to be done too, then. Commentary finished. Mission accomplished.

But it can also feel like a disappointing place to stop. After all, at the end of 2 Samuel, David is still alive, and we might want to know what else happened to him in his life. At the end of 2 Samuel, David also doesn't have a successor, so it's unclear where the story will go after his death. There are other characters as well, whom we may have grown interested in, but who don't have satisfying conclusions either. We have stories about all this stuff, but not until the first chapters of the next book of the Bible, 1 Kings.

If you want to stop now, you'd be in good company. Some biblical scholars will insist on stopping now, believing that whoever wrote the first two chapters of 1 Kings was someone very different from whoever wrote 1 and 2 Samuel. If we do stop now, we might not get a conventional end to David's story, but we do stop on something of a high note. David has just had a big breakthrough about personal responsibility. It's a teachable moment. From time to time, we could all benefit from the reminder to stop blaming people around us and focus on recognizing, confessing, and improving our own faults. David's last words would be a pious plea. Not a bad way to go.

But if you want to press on, I can't blame you. Some biblical scholars would insist on that as well. Just around the corner we get resolutions for multiple characters and plot lines, and we reconnect again with the rest of the overarching history of Israel and Judah. The price for going on is a very different end for David. David's last words won't be pious anymore—they'll be violent and bitter. Perhaps that's the David you've had in mind all along, and so it's no loss for you. Perhaps you'd rather remember him as he was in 2 Samuel 24.

Whatever the case might be, in the interest of thoroughness, this commentary on 1 and 2 Samuel will cheat just a bit and go on to the first two chapters of 1 Kings.

Let's see what we get.

Bathsheba vs. Joab (1 Kings 1–2)

In the final months of David's life, he succumbs to failing health and impotency, and has yet to declare a successor. His oldest son Adonijah, with support from the commander Joab and Eli's descendent Abiathar, declares himself king. But the prophet Nathan conspires with Bathsheba to have her son Solomon put on the throne instead. Taking advantage of his declining mental state, Bathsheba persuades David to give Solomon his support. Benaiah, captain of David's special forces, and Zadok the priest get behind Solomon, allowing him to outmaneuver his way to the throne.

With Solomon made king, David's last words become a list of people Solomon ought to kill to consolidate his power. Abiathar is exiled, Adonijah and Shimei (the guy who insulted David when he fled Jerusalem) are killed, and Joab meets his end in the sanctuary at the hands of Solomon's new general, Benaiah.

David then dies.

Bathsheba

The story opens with palace intrigue. We're given two examples of David's advanced age and failing health: he can't get warm no matter how many blankets he's given (1 Kings 1:2), and even when he's provided with Abishag, the most beautiful virgin in the land, he isn't able to sleep with her (1:3–4). The virility of men in Ancient West Asia was an important indicator of their worthiness to lead and of their divine favor. When David isn't able to respond to Abishag, it becomes obvious to everyone that they need to prepare for a contested succession.

Adonijah, David's oldest son and the ostensible heir, makes the first move. Like Absalom before him, he gets himself horses, a chariot, and men to run alongside him (1:5). Also like Absalom, he's very attractive (1:6b). The narrator inserts an interesting note about how Adonijah only makes a play for the throne because he was never discouraged by David from doing so (1:6a). We never got a comment like this about Absalom, despite his run for king being a monumental disaster. This recognition of the role of David's parenting in shaping the character of his sons is belated but important.

Adonijah secures the support of Joab and Abiathar, who represent the military and the priesthood, respectively, then he offers a mass sacrifice in front of all the royal officials (1:7, 9), much like David did after he moved his capital to Jerusalem. With those steps taken, it looks like he has the throne well in hand.

But the prophet Nathan has a different agenda. He goes to Bathsheba and devises a plan to double-team David in private (1:11–14). Bathsheba sweeps into David's room and says, "Hey, didn't you swear that Solomon would be king?" (1:15–21). And then Nathan barges in and says, "Hey, why is Adonijah king?" (1:22–27). They overwhelm the frail David, and he immediately capitulates.

Nathan anoints Solomon and they put him on the king's mule with Benaiah (representing the army) and Zadok (representing the priesthood) in support (1:32–40). When the mounted Solomon comes marching through the city with the king's horns blaring and the people cheering, Adonijah and his supporters flee (1:41–53).

I should note that, although Nathan is a prophet and prefers Solomon as king, we're not told in this story that God told Nathan to prefer Solomon. It would be both unwise and unbiblical to presume that, just because a prophet is speaking, they're speaking on behalf of God. Without a line like "The Lord told Nathan to say X," it reads like Nathan has personal motivations for preferring Solomon over Adonijah.

And what could his motivations be? It seems unlikely that he wanted Solomon to be king because of prophetic insight into his future rule. While Solomon is described as enormously wise and wealthy, he also enslaves his own people, commits idolatry, and is himself such a terrible father that the pride of his son Rehoboam results in the permanent severance of the united monarchy into Israel in the north and Judah in the south. Unfortunately, whatever motivations he had are lost to history.

Bathsheba's motivations are much clearer, however. As we have seen before, a common fate of the women in a king's household is to be used as sexual props by future claimants to the throne. If Adonijah became king, Bathsheba's son Solomon will almost certainly be executed, and she'll be passed off into the hands of Adonijah or one of his favored officials. This is obviously an unacceptable option for her.

Since Solomon does become king, and since Bathsheba is instrumental in that happening, it's really Bathsheba in the end whose voice shapes the future of the kingdom. While her introduction to the story began with victimization and powerlessness, it ends as happily as one could hope, with her in a safe position of power.

Bathsheba takes one more step to secure Solomon's rule. After he's on the throne, Adonijah comes to Bathsheba and asks her if Solomon will give him Abishag, the beautiful virgin and last concubine of David (2:13–18). This is a really, really, really stupid thing for Adonijah to do. He is asking one of the key architects of the opposition party to do something that would effectively move him closer to the throne. There's no way Bathsheba would help Adonijah accomplish this. All Bathsheba has to do is relate Adonijah's request to Solomon, and Solomon has Adonijah killed (2:19–25).

The death of Adonijah marks the ultimate fulfillment of the consequences David unknowingly posed when confronted by Nathan. When Nathan told David the story of a wealthy man stealing a prized possession from a poor man, David declared the wealthy man should have to give back four-fold of what he took. David took one life, Uriah's, so he had to pay it back with four lives: his unnamed child with Bathsheba, Amnon, Absalom, and Adonijah.

Joab

Joab is first discussed in 1 Kings 1:7 as a supporter of Adonijah along with Abiathar the priest. Speaking of motivations, it's quite strange that Joab and Abiathar, two of David's most loyal supporters who had been with him since he was on the run from Saul, chose against Nathan and Bathsheba to back Adonijah. Unfortunately, again, the text provides no answer for this. Given that Solomon ends up with many of David's weaknesses with respect to fatherhood, women, and his (lack of) appreciation for those beneath him, perhaps Joab and Abiathar saw something different in Adonijah. We can't know.

David's last words to Solomon are of two very different kinds. For three verses, David offers his son moral platitudes about being a man and doing what God says (2:2–4). It's late and vague advice, but it's still a positive example of David exhorting a child to something worthwhile.

Then, for five verses, David explains to Solomon whom he should kill and why (2:5–9).

Shimei is an obvious choice, the guy who insulted David when he was fleeing from Jerusalem. Abishai, Joab's brother, offered to kill Shimei twice, and David got upset with him for always being so violent. I guess in the end, David was persuaded that Abishai had it right all along.

Abiathar is also dealt with, removed from the priesthood and effectively condemned to house arrest (2:26). Solomon says Abiathar deserves to die, but he spares him because Abiathar carried the ark of the covenant. When Abiathar's fate is described, the narrator reminds us that this was all because he is a descendent of Eli (2:27).

Joab, though, is less obvious. David advises Solomon to kill Joab because he feels the deaths of Abner and Amasa burdened him with innocent blood (2:5–6). Here, David regresses back to failing to take responsibility for the things he's done.[11] Neither Abner nor Amasa was innocent. Both were rival generals—Abner tried to usurp the northern throne, and Amasa led a civil war against David. The nonsensical nature of David's reasoning implies his motivation is something else.

---

[11] I said you might want to stop at the end of 2 Samuel.

The most realistic thing we can point to in the narrative is Joab's killing of Absalom and his public chastisement of David afterwards.

Perhaps David just didn't want to die knowing Joab, his life-long enforcer, was otherwise going to the grave in peace while David himself had to lose so much along the way. That sounds like him. Whatever the case might be, David then "goes the way of all the Earth" and dies.

Benaiah, commander of the Philistine mercenaries, is sent to eliminate Joab. Joab flees to the sanctuary (2:28). It's possible he thought he'd be safe there, as it did briefly save Adonijah's life when he did the same thing. Benaiah tells Joab to come out, but Joab decides to die there. When this is reported back to Solomon, he is persistent and tells Benaiah to go inside to kill Joab (2:29–34).

It's hard for me to believe that Joab couldn't have just killed Benaiah. After all, he is undefeated and has killed other commanders in one-on-one fights. But Joab's attitude toward the end seems to be one of capitulation. Lifelong loyalty to God's anointed hasn't paid off for him. He's giving up. He's fought enough. Once he's dead, the war machine marches on, and Benaiah is put over the army in his place.

There's always another king and another general to take the lives in his way.

So What?

Aristotle defined tragedy as a genre where a depiction of events evokes fear and pity for the purposes of cleansing those same feelings. I don't think it's a stretch to say that 1 and 2 Samuel evokes fear and pity. Terrifying things regularly happen to innocent people, and we are often moved to pity by the suffering of those same characters.

You might even feel pity of a slightly different kind for the characters causing that suffering. You might pity Saul, though he murders many, because of the way Samuel has it out for him and because an evil spirit of God torments him. You might pity David, though he is guilty of a laundry list of sins, because he loses four children and spends his last days as a pawn in other people's plays for the throne.

Are we cleansed of those feelings by the story's end? That's possible. You might also feel tired, frustrated, and disappointed. Totally valid.

The story of 1 and 2 Samuel is also a tragedy in the more basic sense that hardly anyone has a happy ending. Hannah does. Originally mourning her childlessness, she's given a son by divine intervention and then wisely departs the story before anything else can happen to her. Bathsheba probably does. She enters the story as a victim and exits as a kingmaker. Anonymous women like the "witch" of Endor, the wise woman of Tekoa, and the wise woman of Beth Maacah are put in life-threatening situations but manage to make it out alive. That's a happy ending of a kind.

But most of the male characters, despite having enormous amounts of power, have the worst endings. Eli begins the story as a priest of authority, but because of his corrupt sons, his household is condemned to extinction. Samuel begins as a prophet with unprecedented access to God, but because of *his* corrupt sons, the Israelites undergo a radical shift to a monarchy with questionable results. He's not even safe from his legacy of failure in the afterlife.

Saul begins the story as the son of a wealthy man, who becomes king and defends his kingdom; then, he fails tests he couldn't possibly pass and is tormented by God into spending his later years as a violent psychopath. David begins the story as nothing but becomes the most powerful and beloved person in the country; and then, because of his sins and the sins he's passed on to his sons, he has to spend his later years putting down rebellions and holding together a fractured kingdom.

Who else? Saul's many sons, Jonathan and Ishbaal included? Dead. David's sons Amnon, his unnamed infant son, Absalom, Adonijah? Dead. Joab? Dead.

It's because of the tragic genre of 1 and 2 Samuel that this commentary has taken a critical approach, making scathing observations and asking hard questions about its characters. After all, if things aren't working out well for them, then we should be cautious about what we're taking away from these stories lest we ruin our own lives with their mistakes.

There are two topics in particular we have been tracking since the introduction: fatherhood and ambivalence. Now that the story is done and its tragic arc has been revealed, let's give a few closing remarks.

Fatherhood

Because of the intergenerational nature of 1 and 2 Samuel's narratives, and because of their close focus on their cast of characters, we get to see several father-child relationships. Most of these, including the most prominent ones, are bad. Before we go any further, we should give two caveats. First, it's entirely possible for a good father to have bad children. Second, it's entirely possible for the fathers in the stories of 1 and

2 Samuel to have been better "off camera," during gaps between the stories the biblical texts choose to tell. Having said that, these caveats aren't enough to excuse what we do see.

If we want to take away something helpful about how to be a good parent/guardian in general, or a good father in particular, we're going to have to treat the characters as negative examples. That is to say, we will aspire to do the opposite of what they do, because what they do leads to family breakdown, immorality, regret, and the harsh judgment of God.

Eli, Samuel, and David appear to suffer from the same problem—a fear of adequately disciplining their children. "Discipline" can take a variety of forms and doesn't need to be punitive or physical. Hurting children we claim to love when they do something wrong only forces them to internalize the idea that love entails pain. That's how you get characters like Amnon, for whom the line between "love" and "hate" is as thin as his own guilty conscience.

But contra Eli, Samuel, and David, discipline should consistently make clear what's wrong while both modeling and incentivizing what's right. Eli only warns his children; he doesn't incentivize a better way. Samuel isn't consistent; he spends all his time traveling for work. And David doesn't model better behavior; rather, he models the evil his children go on to repeat.

All three characters are also at a considerable emotional distance from their children; they have little idea what's happening in their children's lives, and they often have to rely on second-hand reporting to know what their children are doing. When they do respond to their children, they show little to no emotional intelligence. David is particularly guilty of this, always feeling the least helpful feels, such that even his most loyal servants don't think he cares about them. The better we know what our children are feeling, and the better we can manage and articulate our own feelings, the better the position we'll be in to help our children and discipline them when necessary.

When God's version of fatherhood involves only punishment, that punishment is inconsistent and difficult to understand. And when

God's presence in 1 and 2 Samuel is only irregularly made known, it's no wonder human characters reflect the same inadequacies. In fact, it's likely the other way around. The human authors of the text, having a very limited conception of what a father could be, projected this kind of fatherhood on God. The healthier our conceptions of fatherhood, the better position we're in to imagine the hypothetical perfect fatherhood of God. But obviously these biblical characters are in no position to do that.

There's nothing in 1 and 2 Samuel about consistently modeling and incentivizing what's right in relation to being a father. as opposed to being any other kind of parent or mentor. What makes being a father unique is that we are trying to parent through the lens of masculinity that our society has provided for us, and so we must parent while trying to overcome the worst parts of masculinity while embracing the good parts. Characters like David spend most of their lives trapped in the worst parts of a toxic masculinity, and it's almost impossible to be a good father from there. The more conscientious we are about what kind of masculinity we're inheriting from our own fathers and our wider culture, the better able we will be to make something good of it to hand down to later generations.

Ambivalence

The relationship between God's will and the unfolding events of history is not easy to parse out. In 1 and 2 Samuel, we have characters who are chosen by God, directed by God, and given victory by God to change history. But we also have characters who are chosen by God yet who are condemned as though they've been doing everything wrong all along.

David probably felt pretty chosen in 1 Samuel 16 when he was anointed by Samuel, or in 2 Samuel 7 when Nathan told him God was guaranteeing him a descendent on the throne forever. David probably felt a lot less chosen when Nathan showed up five chapters later to tell him the sword would never depart from his house, and even less chosen when he held the bodies of his dead heirs in his arms. And then there's us, reading this all, being like, "What is God doing?"

When we examine our own situations in history, we might wonder whether or not the things that are happening are also things God is choosing or directing. Is God behind the scenes picking leaders of countries? Is God determining the outcome of events? Do conflicts between nations ultimately come down to who God wants to win? In the face of these difficult-to-answer questions, it's easy to find ourselves feeling uncertain or apathetic, or holding contradictory ideas.

The disadvantages of ambivalence are easy to see. The statement "I definitely know whose side God is on here" is virtually impossible to justify even when looking at the biblical texts where that answer should be closest to the surface. Wouldn't it be nice to know? It might be. Except that, when characters know which side God is on, they can abuse that knowledge and muddle God's cause with selfish ambitions.

But the less obvious advantage of ambivalence is worth noting as well. Because the statement "I definitely know whose side God is on here" is impossible to justify, the only way we can approach an answer is in conversation with other people. We have to read biblical texts together; we have to examine history and current events together; and we have to bring our many unanswered questions together. Ambivalence is fertile ground for the growth of relationships as we share and listen to the ideas of others in pursuit of a common understanding.

After all, you're here, reading this book! You wanted to know more, and whether or not you are reading alone, you're coming into contact with a massive transhistorical conversation about God and history. Here, your curiosities are valuable, and your contributions are welcome. Ambivalence makes space for you.

Constructive Theology

Most of this commentary is written for a broad audience who could come from any religious or non-religious background. Comments about the nature of God have been limited, and I fully believe the stories in 1 and 2 Samuel can be appreciated in many different ways, regardless of whether God exists or whether any particular religion is true.

What comments have been made, have been from the perspective of "biblical theology," where I've tried to articulate what the biblical authors thought of God. The comments haven't concerned what a faith tradition today believes about God (that would be "dogmatic theology") or what might be true about God in the most comprehensive sense (that would be "systematic theology").

But for those who come to 1 and 2 Samuel wanting to know more about God, I don't want to leave you hanging. I'll offer a few thoughts from the perspective of a mainline Methodist Christian. These are limited and intentionally selective comments, which are inspired by the text but aren't necessarily representative of what the biblical authors themselves might have thought, and so they are best classified as "constructive theology."

Two things really strike me when reading 1 and 2 Samuel. The first is the peculiar nature of sin. While sin abounds in both life and the stories in 1 and 2 Samuel, it's not evenly distributed. Consistently, it is women characters who are both the victims of men's sin and the ones who bear the consequences of men's sin. Women are hurt and then hurt again as a consequence of the first hurt. Unfortunately, this continues to be a feature of life today. While some societies around the world have made enormous strides toward becoming more egalitarian, systemic sexism and interpersonal misogyny continue to exist, in these societies and others, some 3,000 years after the time period in which 1 and 2 Samuel were set.

When reflecting on these stories, it's clear that sin is disproportionately perpetrated by the powerful against the powerless. And insofar as God can't abide sin, this means that God is disproportionately aligned with the powerless. This is why, in Christian tradition, when God walks the Earth, God does so in the form of the powerless. Paul says,

Let the same mind be in you that was in Christ Jesus, though he existed in the form of God, did not regard equality with God as something to be grasped, but emptied himself, taking the form of a slave, assuming human likeness. And being found in appearance as a human, he humbled himself and became obedient to the point of death—even death on a cross. (Philipians 2:5-8 NRSVue)

God could have come as a king, but God did not. While the gospel is good news for all because the end of sin is good for all, it is better news for those who have suffered most egregiously as a result of sin. God's ultimate delivery of justice is most sweet to those who have been crying out for it, not for those who have caused the cry.

The second thing that really strikes me is the transformational potential of confession in loving relationships. Some of the most poignant moments in these stories of kings and their wars are small, intimate conversations between two people. I have in mind Jonathan and David (1 Samuel 20:41–42), Saul and David (1 Samuel 24:8–22), Joab and David (2 Samuel 19:1–8), and God and David (2 Samuel 24:17).

Each of these relationships was loving at one point. Jonathan loved David as his own soul (1 Samuel 18:1) and David loved Jonathan with more love than he had for women (2 Samuel 1:26). Saul was said to love David (1 Samuel 16:21). Joab implies that he loves David (2 Samuel 19:6). And David is supposed to be a "man after God's own heart" (1 Samuel 13:14). It's in these quiet moments between characters that they become aware of truths about their purpose in the world; it's where they make oaths that ought to bind their behavior moving forward or where they turn away from past behavior if only for a moment.

These characters often fail to live up to who they are in these moments, just as we all fail to live up to who we are in our best moments. But that makes these moments all the more important. The motivation of love and the safety of a relationship help us see beyond ourselves toward what we might be. And with that goal perceived, we can strive toward it.

Christianity is a religion of confession, where the drama of recognizing and articulating sins is matched only by the drama of the forgiveness of those sins. This is why 1 John 1:8–10 insists we have all sinned and assures us that God will forgive us when we confess those sins. This is why James 5:16 encourages us to confess our sins to one another. Confession makes transformation possible, here in part, ultimately in whole.

Confession is how we can turn a tragedy into victory.

The men in 1 and 2 Samuel are some of the most toxic people in the Bible. They tried and they failed.

Let's try to do better.

Things for Normal People to Read or Watch (Or Not...No Judgment)

General Resources for Academic Approaches to the Hebrew Bible

Collins, John. *A Short Introduction to the Hebrew Bible*. Minneapolis: Fortress Press, 2018.

Coogan, Michael, Marc Brettler, Carol Newsom, and Pheme Perkins, eds. *The New Oxford Annotated Study Bible with Apocrypha: New Revised Standard Version*. Oxford: Oxford University Press, 2018.

Hayes, Christine. "Introduction to the Old Testament on Yale Open Courses." Introduction to the Old Testament (Hebrew Bible) | Open Yale Courses (https://oyc.yale.edu/religious-studies/rlst-145)

Finkelstein, Israel and Neil Asher Silberman. *The Bible Unearthed: Archeology's New Vision of Ancient Israel and the Origin of Its Sacred Texts*. New York: The Free Press, 2002.

Resources for the Further Study of 1 and 2 Samuel

Bach, Alice, ed. *Women in the Hebrew Bible: A Reader*. Oxfordshire: Routledge, 2013.

Brenner-Idan, Athalya, ed. *A Feminist Companion to Samuel and Kings*. Sheffield: Sheffield Academic Press, 1994.

Brueggemann, Walter. *First and Second Samuel: Interpretation: A Bible Commentary for Teaching and Preaching.* Westminster John Knox Press: Louisville, 1990.

Gafney, Wil. *Womanist Midrash: A Reintroduction to the Women of the Torah and the Throne.* Louisville: Westminster John Knox Press, 2017.

Jobling, David. *Berit Olam: 1 Samuel.* Collegeville: Liturgical Press, 1998

Sweeney, Marvin. *1-2 Samuel* (New Cambridge Commentary). Cambridge: Cambridge University Press, 2023.

Van Wijk-Bos, Joanna W.H. *The Road to Kingship: 1-2 Samuel.* Grand Rapids: Eerdmans, 2020

Resources for the Study of King David and his World

Baden, Joel. *The Historical David: The Real Life of an Invented Hero.* New York: Harper Collins, 2013.

Halbertal, Moshe and Stephen Holmes. *The Beginning of Politics: Power in the Biblical Book of Samuel.* Princeton: Princeton University Press, 2019.

Halpern, Baruch. *David's Secret Demons: Messiah, Murderer, Traitor, King.* Grand Rapids: Wm. B. Eerdmans, 2003.

Jennings, Ted. *Jacob's Wound: Homoerotic Narrative in the Literature of Ancient Israel.* London: Continuum, 2005.

Wolpe, David. *David: The Divided Heart.* New Haven: Yale University Press, 2014.

Forthcoming

Higashi, Aaron. *1 and 2 Chronicles for Normal People: A Guide to the Boldest but Least Popular Books of the Bible.* 2025

About this Book

About the Author

Dr. Aaron Higashi is an adjunct instructor at Grand Canyon University. He received his B.A. in philosophy from the University of Colorado at Colorado Springs (2008), his M.A. in biblical studies from Providence College (2010), his S.T.M. from Chicago Theological Seminary (2011), and his Ph.D. in Bible, culture, and hermeneutics with an emphasis in Hebrew Bible from Chicago Theological Seminary (2021). Aaron is interested in the relationship between ideology, moral philosophy, and biblical interpretation, and shares biblical scholarship with a popular audience @abhbible on TikTok. Aaron lives in Scottsdale, Arizona with his pediatrician wife and three young daughters, where he does jiu-jitsu, drinks too much coffee, plays video games, and tries to discuss biblical interpretation at parties and other social events where it's probably not cool to do so.

Behind the Scenes

Publishing Director Lauren O'Connell
Editor Caroline Blyth
Cover Design Danny Wong

Enjoyed this Book?

Head over to thebiblefornormalpeople.com/join to join the Society of Normal People, where you can:

- access all of our classes and courses,
- connect with other "normal people,"
- enjoy sneak peaks into upcoming projects,
- have conversations with The Bible for Normal People team,
- *and* get podcast exclusives, including access to an ad-free stream.

Or follow us on Facebook and Instagram (@thebiblefornormalpeople) for more The Bible for Normal People content.